C# EDITION

Building Maintainable Software
Ten Guidelines for Future-Proof Code

Joost Visser

Beijing · Boston · Farnham · Sebastopol · Tokyo

Building Maintainable Software, C# Edition

by Joost Visser

Printed in the United States of America.

Published by O'Reilly Media, Inc., 1005 Gravenstein Highway North, Sebastopol, CA 95472.

O'Reilly books may be purchased for educational, business, or sales promotional use. Online editions are also available for most titles (*http://safaribooksonline.com*). For more information, contact our corporate/institutional sales department: 800-998-9938 or *corporate@oreilly.com*.

Editors: Nan Barber and Rachel Roumeliotis
Production Editor: Colleen Cole
Copyeditor: Nan Barber
Indexer: WordCo Indexing Services, Inc.

Interior Designer: David Futato
Cover Designer: Karen Montgomery
Illustrator: Rebecca Demarest

April 2016:   First Edition

Revision History for the First Edition
2016-04-18:   First Release

See *http://oreilly.com/catalog/errata.csp?isbn=9781491954522* for release details.

978-1-491-95452-2

[LSI]

Table of Contents

About the Authors

Joost Visser is Head of Research at the Software Improvement Group. In this role, he is responsible for the science behind the methods and tools that SIG offers to measure and master software. Joost also holds a position as professor of Large-Scale Software Systems at Radboud University Nijmegen. He has obtained his PhD in Computer Science from the University of Amsterdam and has published over 100 papers on topics such as generic programming, program transformation, green computing, software quality, and software evolution. Joost considers software engineering a socio-technical discipline, and he is convinced that software measurement is essential for development teams and product owners to thrive.

Pascal van Eck joined the Software Improvement Group in 2013 as a general consultant on software quality. Prior to joining SIG, for 13 years Pascal was Assistant Professor of Information Systems at University of Twente, The Netherlands. Pascal holds a PhD in Computer Science from Vrije Universiteit Amsterdam and has published over 80 papers in areas such as enterprise architecture, IT security, and software metrics. Pascal is chairman of the program committee of the Dutch National Conference on Architecture for the Digital World.

After obtaining an MSc degree in Software Engineering from Delft University of Technology in 2005, **Rob van der Leek** joined SIG as a software quality consultant. Working at SIG is for Rob the closest thing to being a software doctor. In his role as a consultant, he combines his thorough technical knowledge on software engineering and software technologies to advise clients on how to keep their systems in shape. Next to being a consultant, Rob fulfills a leading role in SIG's internal development team. This team develops and maintains the company's software analysis tooling. It's Rob's ambition to leave the IT industry a bit better than he found it.

Sylvan Rigal has worked as a software quality consultant at SIG since 2011 and has advised clients on managing their IT since 2008. He helps clients achieve lower software maintenance costs and enhanced security by prioritizing improvements in software design and development processes. He holds a MSc in international business from Maastricht University, The Netherlands. As an active member of SIG's software security team, Sylvan trains consultants on analyzing software security risks. When he is not assessing the technical health of software, he is training in Brazilian jiu jitsu, enjoying Amsterdam's restaurants, or traveling through Asia. Approximately in that order.

Gijs Wijnholds joined the Software Improvement Group in 2015 as a software quality consultant in public administration. He helps clients get in control of their software projects by advising them on development processes and translating technical risks into strategic decisions. Gijs holds a BSc in AI from Utrecht University and a MSc degree in Logic from the University of Amsterdam. He is an expert on Haskell and mathematical linguistics.

Preface

In der Beschränkung zeigt sich erst der Meister. (In simplicity one recognizes true skill.)
  —J.W. von Goethe

After 15 years of consulting about software quality, we at the Software Improvement Group (SIG) have learned a thing or two about maintainability.

First, insufficient maintainability is a real problem in the practice of software development. Low maintainability means that developers spend too much time on maintaining and fixing old code. That leaves less time available for the most rewarding part of software development: writing new code. Our experience, as well as the data we have collected, shows that maintaining source code takes at least twice as long when maintainability is measured as below average, compared to when maintainability is above average. See Appendix A to learn how we measure maintainability.

Second, lack of maintainability is to a large extent caused by simple issues that occur over and over again. Consequently, the most efficient and effective way to improve maintainability is to address these simple issues. Improving maintainability does not require magic or rocket science. A combination of relatively simple skills and knowledge, plus the discipline and environment to apply them, leads to the largest improvement in maintainability.

At SIG, we have seen systems that are essentially unmaintainable. In these systems, bugs are not fixed, and functionality is not changed or extended because it is considered too time-consuming and risky. Unfortunately, this is all too common in today's IT industry, but it does not have to be like that.

That is why we have written the 10 guidelines. We want to share the knowledge and skills that any practicing software developer should master to consistently write maintainable source code. We are confident that after reading and understanding the 10 guidelines, as a software developer you will be able to write maintainable source code. What is left, then, is the environment to apply these skills to maximum effect, including shared development practices, appropriate tooling, and more. We cover these development environment essentials in a second book, called *Building Software Teams*.

The Topic of This Book: Ten Guidelines for Building Maintainable Software

The guidelines in the following chapters are independent of the type of system. The guidelines are about the size and number of parameters in units of code (methods in C#), the number of decision points, and other properties of source code. They are well-known guidelines that many programmers may have heard about in their training. The chapters also provide examples, mostly in the form of refactoring patterns, of how to apply the guidelines in practice. Although the guidelines are presented in C#, they are independent of the programming language used. Eight out of 10 of them are derived from the SIG/TÜViT[1] Evaluation Criteria for Trusted Product Maintainability,[2] a set of metrics to systematically rate source code maintainability.

Why You Should Read This Book

Taken in isolation, the guidelines presented in this book are well known. In fact, many commonly used tools for code analysis check a number of the guidelines presented here. For instance, Checkstyle (*http://checkstyle.sourceforge.net*) (Java), Style-Cop+ (*http://stylecopplus.codeplex.com*) (for C#), Pylint (*http://www.pylint.org*) (for Python), JSHint (*http://jshint.com*) (for JavaScript), RuboCop (*https://github.com/bbat sov/rubocop*) (for Ruby), and PMD (*https://pmd.github.io*) (covers multiple languages, including C# and Java) all check compliance with the guideline presented in Chapter 2. The following three characteristics, however, set this book apart from other books on software development:

We have selected the 10 most important guidelines from experience
> Style guides and static code analysis tools can be daunting. Checkstyle version 6.9 contains some 150 rules, each of which implies a guideline. They all make sense, but their effect on maintainability is not equal. We have selected the 10 guideline chapters because they have the highest impact on maintainability. The box "Why These Ten Specific Guidelines?" on page xi explains how we have chosen our guidelines.

---

1 TÜViT is part of TÜV, a worldwide organization of German origin for technical quality management. It specializes in certification and consulting for IT in general and security in particular.

2 See Maintainability Evaluation Criteria. (*http://bit.ly/eval_criteria*)

We teach how to comply with these 10 guidelines

Stating *what* a programmer should or should not do is one thing (and many style guides do just that). Providing guidance on *how* to comply with the guidelines is another. In this book, for each guideline we provide concrete examples of how to build code that complies with it.

We present statistics and examples from real-world systems

At SIG, we have seen a *lot* of source code made by real-world programmers under real-world constraints. That source code contains compromises. Therefore, we are sharing data from our benchmark to show how real-world source code compares with the guidelines.

Who Should Read This Book

This book is aimed at software developers who know how to program in C#. We distinguish between two groups of such developers. The first group comprises developers who received comprehensive training in computer science or software engineering (e.g., by majoring in one of those fields in college or university). For those developers, our book should reinforce basic principles that they have been taught in introductory programming courses.

The second group comprises software developers who entered the field without any comprehensive training in computer science or software engineering. We are thinking of developers who are self-taught, or who majored in a totally different field in college or university and then made a career switch. Our experience is that this group often received very little training beyond the syntax and semantics of the programming language they are using. This is the group for whom we have specifically written.

Why These Ten Specific Guidelines?

This book presents 10 guidelines. The first eight have a one-to-one relationship with the so-called *system properties* in the SIG/TÜViT Evaluation Criteria Trusted Product Maintainability, which underpins the way SIG rates maintainability. For the SIG/TÜViT evaluation criteria, we have selected metrics that:

- Are contained in a set as small as possible
- Are technology-independent
- Are easy to measure
- Enable a meaningful comparison of real-world enterprise software systems

The eight system properties that comprise the SIG/TÜViT evaluation criteria are the result of this selection. To those we have added two process guidelines (regarding

---

clean code and automation) that we consider to be the most critical and under your direct control.

Researchers in computer science and software engineering have been prolific in defining source code metrics. Depending on how you count, tens if not hundreds of different metrics have been reported. So the eight system properties that we apply are clearly not the complete set of maintainability metrics.

We argue, however, that the eight SIG/TÜViT metrics are both adequate and sufficient to measure maintainability, as they solve the following problems:

Metrics that are technology dependent
> Some metrics (e.g., depth of inheritance) are applicable only to source code in particular technologies (e.g., only in object-oriented languages). While dominant in practice, object orientation is far from the only technology. There is still a lot of non-object-oriented source code out there (think of systems in Cobol, RPG, C, and Pascal) that we need to cover in our maintainability assessments.

Metrics that are strongly correlated to other metrics
> Some metrics are known to have a strong correlation to other metrics. An example is the total number of decision points in a system. There is empirical evidence that this metric is strongly correlated to code volume. This means that once you know the total number of lines of code in the system (which is easy to measure), you can predict the number of decision points with high certainty. It makes no sense to include the less easy-to-measure metric: you would have the additional burden of executing the measurement and reporting its outcome, but it would tell you nothing that you could not derive from the easier metric.

Metrics that do not differentiate in practice
> Some metrics are defined in a theoretically sound way, but in the practice of software development, all systems score more or less the same. It makes no sense to include these in an assessment model, as systems cannot be distinguished on the outcome of such a metric.

What This Book Is Not

This book uses C# (and only C#) to illustrate and explain our guidelines. Yet it does not teach C# in itself. We assume that the reader is at least able to read C# and the API of the standard libraries that come with it. We have tried to keep the code examples simple, using basic features of the language.

This is also not a book about C# idioms—that is, about C#-specific conventions on how to express functionality in code. We do not believe that you achieve maintainability by using specific language-dependent idiom. To the contrary, the guidelines presented here are to a very large extent language-independent, and therefore also independent of language idioms.

While we introduce and explain a number of refactoring patterns, what follows is not meant to be a comprehensive catalogue of such patterns. There are already books and websites out there that are very good pattern catalogues. Our book focuses on *why* and *how* a number of selected refactoring patterns contribute to maintainability. Therefore, this book serves as a stepping stone for such catalogues.

The Follow-up Book

We know that individual developers do not control all parts of the development process. Which development tools are used, how quality control is organized, how deployment pipelines are set up, and so on are all important factors that influence software quality but are also a *team* responsibility. Those topics are therefore outside the scope of this book. We do discuss them in a follow-up book, *Building Software Teams*. That book deals with discussing best practices in that field and how to measure their implementation.

About the Software Improvement Group

Although the front cover lists one name, the *real* author of this book is much more than just one person. The real author is SIG, a software management consulting company. That is, the book consolidates the collective experience and knowledge of the SIG consultants that have been measuring software quality and advising about it since 2000. We run a unique, certified,[3] software analysis laboratory that performs standardized inspections against the ISO 25010 international standard for software product quality.

One of the services provided by SIG is our Software Risk Monitoring service. Our clients using this service upload their source code at regular intervals (usually once a week). These uploads are then automatically inspected in our software analysis laboratory. Anything out of the ordinary detected by this automatic analysis is then assessed by SIG consultants and discussed with the client. At the time of writing, in total SIG has analyzed 7.1 billion lines of code, and 72.7 million new lines of code are uploaded to SIG weekly.

SIG was established in 2000. Its roots can be traced back to the Dutch National Research Institute for Mathematics and Computer Science (*Centrum voor Wiskunde en Informatica* [CWI] in Dutch). Even after 15 years, we still keep and value our links with the academic software engineering research community. SIG consultants regularly contribute to scientific publications, and several PhD theses have been based on research to develop and improve the SIG quality model.

---

3 That is, ISO/IEC 17025 certified.

About This Edition

This is the C# edition of the book. All code examples are in C# (and in C# only), and the text frequently refers to tools and terms that are widely used in the C# community, but not necessarily outside of it. We assume that the reader has experience in C# programming. As previously noted, the guidelines, while presented in this edition in C#, are independent of the programming language used. A Java edition is published concurrently by O'Reilly.

Related Books

We present 10 basic guidelines for achieving high maintainability. While it might be the first book many people will read on the topic of maintainability, we hope it will certainly not be the last one. We recommend several books as follow-up:

Building Software Teams, by the Software Improvement Group
> This is the companion to the current book, written by the same authors. While the current book focuses on developer guidelines for building maintainable software, this book focuses on development process best practices and how to measure them wisely with the Goal-Question-Metric approach. *Building Software Teams* is scheduled for publication in 2016.

Refactoring: Improving the Design of Existing Code, by Martin Fowler
> This book focuses on improving maintainability (and other quality characteristics) of existing code.

Clean Code: A Handbook of Agile Software Craftsmanship, by Robert C. Martin (a.k.a. Uncle Bob)
> Like the current book, *Clean Code* is about building software source code that is of high quality. *Clean Code* describes guidelines at a higher level of abstraction.

Code Quality: The Open Source Perspective, by Diomidis Spinellis
> Also like the current book, *Code Quality* presents guidelines for code quality, but like *Clean Code*, they are presented at a higher level of abstraction.

Design Patterns: Elements of Reusable Object-Oriented Software, by Erich Gamma, Richard Helm, Ralph Johnson, and John Vlissides (a.k.a. the Gang of Four)
> This is recommended reading for those software developers who want to become better software architects.

Conventions Used in This Book

The following typographical conventions are used in this book:

Italic
> Indicates new terms, URLs, email addresses, filenames, and file extensions.

`Constant width`
> Used for program listings, as well as within paragraphs to refer to program elements such as variable or function names, databases, data types, environment variables, statements, and keywords.

This element signifies a tip or suggestion.

This element signifies a general note.

This element indicates a warning or caution.

This element indicates an important remark.

Generic Names for Elements of Source Code

Although in the book we use C# to illustrate maintainability guidelines, these guidelines are not specific to C#. The guidelines are inspired by the SIG maintainability model, which is technology-independent and has been applied to about a hundred programming languages and related technologies (such as JSP).

Programming languages differ in the features they provide and (of course) their syntax. For example, where Java uses the keyword `final` for a constant, C# uses `readonly` for exactly the same thing. As another example, C# provides a feature called *partial classes*, which Java (currently) does not provide.

In addition to differences in syntax, programming languages also differ in the terminology they use in textbooks, tutorials, and their individual specifications. For instance, the concept of a group of code lines that can be executed as a whole is known in almost every programming language. In Java and C#, this concept is called a *method*. In Visual Basic, it is called a *subroutine*. In JavaScript and C, it is known as a *function*. In Pascal, it is known as a *procedure*.

That is why a technology-independent model needs generic names for grouping concepts. Table P-1 presents the generic names that we use throughout the chapters.

Table P-1. A generic grouping of concepts and their representation in C#.

Generic name	Generic definition	In C#
Unit	Smallest grouping of lines that can be executed independently	Method or constructor
Module	Smallest grouping of units	Top-level class, interface, or enum
Component	Top-level division of a system as defined by its software architecture	(Not defined by the language)
System	The entire codebase under study	(Not defined by the language)

The following list further clarifies the relationship between the grouping constructs described in Table P-1 and the practice of C# programming:

From smallest to largest

The grouping concepts in Table P-1 are ordered from smallest to largest. A unit itself consists of statements, but statements are not a grouping construct.

 In C#, as in many other programming languages, there is a complex relationship between statements and lines in the *.cs* file in which they appear. A line may have more than one statement, but a statement can be spread over multiple lines. We simply look at *lines of code* (LoC): any line in source code that ends with an Enter/Return, and neither is empty nor contains only a comment.

Some concepts are not defined in a particular language

As Table P-1 shows, some generic concepts are not represented in C#. For instance, in C# there is no syntax to describe the boundaries of a system. This concept is introduced in the generic terminology because we do need it. It is not a problem that C# lacks the syntax: in practice we have other ways to determine these boundaries.

Some well-known generic concepts play no role

You might be surprised that Table P-1 does not define well-known terms such as *subcomponent* and *subsystem*. The reason is simple: we do not need them for the guidelines.

Not all grouping constructs of a language are represented

C# has more grouping constructs than those listed in Table P-1. C# has namespaces to group classes and interfaces. C# also has nested classes. They are not listed in Table P-1 because we do not need them for the guidelines. For example, we do not need to distinguish between classes and nested classes to formulate our guidelines about coupling.

 A C# namespace is *not* the same as a component in the generic terminology. In very small C# systems, there may be a one-to-one mapping between components and namespaces. In larger C# systems, there are usually far more namespaces than components.

Build tooling plays no role in the generic terminology

In C# development, Visual Studio provides an additional grouping concept: build targets. However, build targets play no role in the guidelines. There may be a one-to-one relation between on the one hand components and on the other hand build targets, but this is not a rule.

Components are determined by the architecture of the system

A component is not a C# concept. Components are neither namespaces nor Visual Studio build targets or solutions. In a given system, there may be a one-to-one mapping between components and Visual Studio projects of solutions, but that is not a rule. Instead, components are the highest-level building blocks as identified by the software architecture of the system. They are the blocks in a "blocks-and-arrows" diagram of the system. Chapter 7 further explains the concept of components and presents some examples.

Using Code Examples

Supplemental material (code examples, exercises, etc.) is available for download at *https://github.com/oreillymedia/building_maintainable_software*.

This book is here to help you get your job done. In general, if example code is offered with this book, you may use it in your programs and documentation. You do not need to contact us for permission unless you're reproducing a significant portion of the code. For example, writing a program that uses several chunks of code from this book does not require permission. Selling or distributing storage media (e.g., CD-ROM) of examples from O'Reilly books does require permission. Answering a question by citing this book and quoting example code does not require permission. Incorporating a significant amount of example code from this book into your product's documentation does require permission.

We appreciate, but do not require, attribution. An attribution usually includes the title, authors, publisher, and ISBN. For example: "*Building Maintainable Software, C# Edition* by Joost Visser. Copyright 2016 Software Improvement Group B.V., 978-1-4919-5452-2."

If you feel your use of code examples falls outside fair use or the permission given above, you may contact us at *permissions@oreilly.com* for special permission.

Safari® Books Online

 *Safari Books Online* is an on-demand digital library that delivers expert content in both book and video form from the world's leading authors in technology and business.

Technology professionals, software developers, web designers, and business and creative professionals use Safari Books Online as their primary resource for research, problem solving, learning, and certification training.

Safari Books Online offers a range of plans and pricing for enterprise, government, education, and individuals.

Members have access to thousands of books, training videos, and prepublication manuscripts in one fully searchable database from publishers like O'Reilly Media, Prentice Hall Professional, Addison-Wesley Professional, Microsoft Press, Sams, Que, Peachpit Press, Focal Press, Cisco Press, John Wiley & Sons, Syngress, Morgan Kaufmann, IBM Redbooks, Packt, Adobe Press, FT Press, Apress, Manning, New Riders, McGraw-Hill, Jones & Bartlett, Course Technology, and hundreds more. For more information about Safari Books Online, please visit us online.

How to Contact Us

Please address comments and questions concerning this book to the publisher:

O'Reilly Media, Inc.
1005 Gravenstein Highway North
Sebastopol, CA 95472
800-998-9938 (in the United States or Canada)
707-829-0515 (international or local)
707-829-0104 (fax)

We have a web page for this book, where we list errata, examples, and any additional information. You can access this page at *http://bit.ly/building_maintainable_soft ware_csharp*.

To comment or ask technical questions about this book, send email to *bookquestions@oreilly.com*.

For more information about our books, courses, conferences, and news, see our website at *http://www.oreilly.com*.

Find us on Facebook: *http://facebook.com/oreilly*

Follow us on Twitter: *http://twitter.com/oreillymedia*

Watch us on YouTube: *http://www.youtube.com/oreillymedia*

Acknowledgments

We would like to thank the following people for writing this book:

- Yiannis Kanellopoulos (SIG) as our project manager, overseeing everything.
- Tobias Kuipers (SIG) as initiator of this project.
- Lodewijk Bergmans (SIG) for helping to develop the book structure.
- Zeeger Lubsen (SIG) for his thorough review.
- Ed Louwers (SIG) for his help with the visuals in this book.
- All SIG (former) employees that are working and have worked on perfecting models for measuring, benchmarking, and interpreting software quality.

From our publisher, O'Reilly:

- Nan Barber as our text reviewer.
- Jay Hilyard as our technical reviewer.

And Arie van Deursen for granting permission to use the JPacman code base.

CHAPTER 1

Introduction

Who wrote this piece of code?? I can't work like this!!

—Any programmer

Being a software developer is great. When someone gives you a problem and requirements, you are able to come up with a solution and translate that solution into a language that a computer understands. These are challenging and rewarding endeavors. Being a software developer can also be a painstaking job. If you regularly have to change source code written by others (or even by yourself), you know that it can be either really easy or really difficult. Sometimes, you can quickly identify the lines of code to change. The change is nicely isolated, and tests confirm that it works as intended. At other times, the only solution is to use a hack that creates more problems than it solves.

The ease or difficulty with which a software system can be modified is known as its *maintainability*. The maintainability of a software system is determined by properties of its source code. This book discusses these properties and presents 10 guidelines to help you write source code that is easy to modify.

In this chapter, we explain what we mean when we speak about maintainability. After that, we discuss why maintainability is important. This sets the stage to introduce the main topic of this book: how to build software that is maintainable from the start. At the end of this introduction we discuss common misunderstandings about maintainability and introduce the principles behind the 10 guidelines presented in this book.

1.1 What Is Maintainability?

Imagine two different software systems that have exactly the same functionality. Given the same input, both compute exactly the same output. One of these two systems is fast and user-friendly, and its source code is easy to modify. The other system is slow and difficult to use, and its source code is nearly impossible to understand, let alone modify. Even though both systems have the same functionality, their quality clearly differs.

Maintainability (how easily a system can be modified) is one characteristic of software quality. Performance (how slow or fast a system produces its output) is another.

The international standard ISO/IEC 25010:2011 (which we simply call ISO 25010 in this book[1]) breaks down software quality into eight characteristics: *maintainability, functional suitability, performance efficiency, compatibility, usability, reliability, security,* and *portability*. This book focuses exclusively on maintainability.

Even though ISO 25010 does not describe how to measure software quality, that does not mean you cannot measure it. In Appendix A, we present how we measure software quality at the Software Improvement Group (SIG) in accordance with ISO 25010.

The Four Types of Software Maintenance

Software maintenance is not about fixing wear and tear. Software is not physical, and therefore it does not degrade by itself the way physical things do. Yet most software systems are modified all the time after they have been delivered. This is what software maintenance is about. Four types of software maintenance can be distinguished:

- Bugs are discovered and have to be fixed (this is called *corrective maintenance*).
- The system has to be adapted to changes in the environment in which it operates—for example, upgrades of the operating system or technologies (this is called *adaptive maintenance*).
- Users of the system (and/or other stakeholders) have new or changed requirements (this is called *perfective maintenance*).
- Ways are identified to increase quality or prevent future bugs from occurring (this is called *preventive maintenance*).

---

1 Full title: *International Standard ISO/IEC 25010. Systems and Software Engineering -- Systems and software Quality Requirements and Evaluation (SQuaRE) -- System and Software Quality Models.* First Edition, 2011-03-01.

1.2 Why Is Maintainability Important?

As you have learned, maintainability is only one of the eight characteristics of software product quality identified in ISO 25010. So why is maintainability so important that it warrants its own, dedicated book? There are two angles to this question:

- Maintainability, or lack thereof, has significant business impact.
- Maintainability is an enabler for other quality characteristics.

Both angles are discussed in the next two sections.

Maintainability Has Significant Business Impact

In software development, the maintenance phase of a software system often spans 10 years or more. During most of this time, there is a continuous stream of issues that need to be resolved (corrective and adaptive maintenance) and enhancement requests that have to be met (perfective maintenance). The efficiency and effectiveness with which issues can be resolved and enhancements can be realized is therefore important for stakeholders.

Maintenance efforts are reduced when issue resolution and enhancements can be performed quickly and easily. If efficient maintenance leads to less maintenance personnel (developers), it also lowers maintenance costs. When the number of developers stays the same, with efficient maintenance they have more time for other tasks, such as building new functionality. Fast enhancements mean shorter time-to-market of new products and services supported by the system. For both issue resolution and enhancements, it holds that if they are slow and troublesome, deadlines may not be met or the system may become unusable.

SIG has collected empirical evidence that issue resolution and enhancements are twice as fast in systems with above-average maintainability than in systems with below-average maintainability. A factor of two is a significant quantity in the practice of enterprise systems. The time it takes to resolve issues and make an enhancement is on the order of days or weeks. It is not the difference between fixing 5 bugs or 10 in an hour; it is the difference between being the first one to the market with a new product, or seeing your competitor months ahead of you.

And that is just the difference between above-average and below-average maintainability. At SIG we have seen newly built systems for which the maintainability was so low that it was no longer possible to effectively modify them—even before the systems went into production. Modifications introduced more bugs than they solved. Development took so long that the business environment (and therefore, user requirements) had already changed. More modifications were needed, which introduced yet more bugs. More often than not, such systems are written off before they ever see a 1.0 release.

Maintainability Is an Enabler for Other Quality Characteristics

Another reason why maintainability is a special aspect of software quality is that it acts as an enabler for other quality characteristics. When a system has high maintainability, it is easier to make improvements in the other quality areas, such as fixing a security bug. More generally speaking, optimizing a software system requires modifications to its source code, whether for performance, functional suitability, security, or any other of the seven nonmaintainability characteristics defined by ISO 25010.

Sometimes they are small, local modifications. Sometimes they involve more invasive restructuring. All modifications require finding a specific piece of source code and analyzing it, understanding its inner logic and its position in the business process that the system facilitates, analyzing dependencies between different pieces of code and testing them, and pushing them through the development pipeline. In any case, in a more maintainable system, these modifications are easier to make, allowing you to implement quality optimizations faster and more effectively. For example, highly maintainable code is more stable than unmaintainable code: changes in a highly maintainable system have fewer unexpected side effects than changes in an entangled system that is hard to analyze and test.

1.3 Three Principles of the Guidelines in This Book

If maintainability is so important, how can you improve maintainability of the code that you write? This book presents 10 guidelines that, if followed, lead to code that is highly maintainable. In the following chapters, each guideline is presented and discussed. In the current chapter, we introduce the principles behind these guidelines:

1. Maintainability benefits most from adhering to simple guidelines.
2. Maintainability is not an afterthought, but should be addressed from the very beginning of a development project. Every individual contribution counts.
3. Some violations are worse than others. The more a software system complies with the guidelines, the more maintainable it is.

These principles are explained next.

Principle 1: Maintainability Benefits Most from Simple Guidelines

People may think that maintainability requires a "silver bullet": one technology or principle that solves maintainability once and for all, *automagically*. Our principle is the very opposite: maintainability requires following simple guidelines that are not sophisticated at all. These guidelines guarantee sufficient maintainability, not perfect maintainability (whatever that may be). Source code that complies with these guidelines can still be made more maintainable. At some point, the additional gains in maintainability become smaller and smaller, while the costs become higher and higher.

Principle 2: Maintainability Is Not an Afterthought, and Every Contribution Counts

Maintainability needs to be addressed from the very start of a development project. We understand that it is hard to see whether an individual "violation" of the guidelines in this book influences the overall maintainability of the system. That is why *all* developers must be disciplined and follow the guidelines to achieve a system that is maintainable overall. Therefore, your individual contribution is of great importance to the whole.

Following the guidelines in this book not only results in more maintainable code, but also sets the right example for your fellow developers. This avoids the "broken windows effect" in which other developers temporarily relax their discipline and take shortcuts. Setting the right example is not necessarily about being the most skilled engineer, but more about retaining discipline during development.

Remember that you are writing code not just for yourself, but also for less-experienced developers that come after you. This thought helps you to simplify the solution you are programming.

Principle 3: Some Violations Are Worse Than Others

The guidelines in this book present metric thresholds as an absolute rule. For instance, in Chapter 2, we tell you to never write methods that have more than 15 lines of code. We are fully aware that in practice, almost always there will be exceptions to the guideline. What if a fragment of source code violates one or more of these guidelines? Many types of tooling for software quality assume that each and every violation is bad. The hidden assumption is that all violations should be resolved. In practice, resolving all violations is neither necessary nor profitable. This all-or-nothing view on violations may lead developers to ignore the violations altogether.

We take a different approach. To keep the metrics simple but also practical, we determine the quality of a complete codebase not by the code's number of violations but by its *quality profiles*. A quality profile divides metrics into distinct categories, ranging from fully compliant code to severe violations. By using quality profiles, we can distinguish moderate violations (for example, a method with 20 lines of code) from severe violations (for example, a method with 200 lines of code). After the next section, which discusses common misunderstandings about maintainability, we explain how quality profiles are used to measure the maintainability of a system.

1.4 Misunderstandings About Maintainability

In this section, we discuss some misunderstandings about maintainability that are encountered in practice.

Misunderstanding: Maintainability Is Language-Dependent

"Our system uses a state-of-the-art programming language. Therefore, it is at least as maintainable as any other system."

The data we have at SIG does not indicate that the technology (programming language) chosen for a system is the dominant determining factor of maintainability. Our dataset contains C# systems that are among the most maintainable, but also, that are among the least maintainable. The average maintainability of all C# systems in our benchmark is itself average, and the same holds for Java. This shows us that it is possible to make very maintainable systems in C# (and in Java), but using either of these languages does not guarantee a system's maintainability. Apparently, there are other factors that determine maintainability.

For consistency, we are using C# code snippets throughout the book. However, the guidelines described in this book are not specific to C#. In fact, SIG has benchmarked systems in over a hundred programming languages based on the guidelines and metrics in this book.

Misunderstanding: Maintainability Is Industry-Dependent

"My team makes embedded software for the car industry. Maintainability is different there."

We believe that the guidelines presented in this book are applicable to all forms of software development: embedded software, games, scientific software, software components such as compilers and database engines, and administrative software. Of course, there are differences between these domains. For example, scientific software often uses a special-purpose programming language, such as R, for statistical analysis. Yet, in R, it is a good idea to keep units short and simple. Embedded software has to operate in an environment where performance predictability is essential and resources are constrained. So whenever a compromise has to be made between performance and maintainability, the former wins over the latter. But no matter the domain, the characteristics defined in ISO 25010 still apply.

Misunderstanding: Maintainability Is the Same as the Absence of Bugs

"You said the system has above-average maintainability. However, it turns out it is full of bugs!"

According to the ISO 25010 definitions, a system can be highly maintainable and still be lacking in other quality characteristics. Consequently, a system may have above-average maintainability and still suffer from problems regarding functional suitability, performance, reliability, and more. Above-average maintainability means nothing more than that the modifications needed to reduce the number of bugs can be made at a high degree of efficiency and effectiveness.

Misunderstanding: Maintainability Is a Binary Quantity

*"My team repeatedly has been able to fix bugs in this system. Therefore, it has been proven that it **is** maintainable."*

This distinction is important. "Maintain-Ability" is literally the ability to maintain. According to its definition in ISO 25010, source code maintainability is not a binary quantity. Instead, maintainability is the degree to which changes can be made efficiently and effectively. So the right question to ask is not whether changes (such as bug fixes) have been made, but rather, how much effort did fixing the bug take (efficiency), and was the bug fixed correctly (effectiveness)?

Given the ISO 25010 definition of maintainability, one could say that a software system is never perfectly maintainable nor perfectly *un*maintainable. In practice, we at SIG have encountered systems that can be considered unmaintainable. These systems had such a low degree of modification efficiency and effectiveness that the system owner could not afford to maintain it.

1.5 Rating Maintainability

We know now that maintainability is a quality characteristic on a scale. It signifies different degrees of being able to maintain a system. But what is "easy to maintain" and what is "hard to maintain"? Clearly, a complex system is easier to maintain by an expert than by a less experienced developer. By benchmarking, at SIG we let the metrics in the software industry answer this question. If software metrics for a system score below average, it is harder than average to maintain. The benchmark is recalibrated yearly. As the industry learns to code more efficiently (e.g., with the help of new technologies), the average for metrics tends to improve over time. What was the norm in software engineering a few years back, may be subpar now. The benchmark thus reflects the state of the art in software engineering.

SIG divides the systems in the benchmark by star rating, ranging from 1 star (hardest to maintain) to 5 stars (easiest to maintain). The distribution of these star ratings among systems from 1 to 5 stars is 5%-30%-30%-30%-5%. Thus, in the benchmark the systems that are among the top 5% are rated 5 stars. In these systems, there are still violations to the guidelines, but much fewer than in systems rated below.

The star ratings serve as a predictor for actual system maintainability. SIG has collected empirical evidence that issue resolution and enhancements are twice as fast in systems with 4 stars than in systems with 2 stars.

The systems in the benchmark are ranked based on their metric quality profiles. Figure 1-1 shows three examples of unit size quality profiles (print readers can view full-color figures for this and the other quality profiles that follow in our repository for this book (*https://github.com/oreillymedia/building_maintainable_software*)).

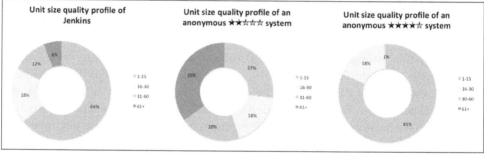

Figure 1-1. Example of three quality profiles

The first chart in Figure 1-1 is a quality profile for unit size based on the source code of Jenkins (*http://jenkins-ci.org/*) version 1.625, a popular open source continuous integration server. The quality profile tells us that the Jenkins codebase has 64% of its code in methods that are no longer than 15 lines of code (compliant with the guideline). The profile also shows that 18% of all the code in the codebase is in methods between 16 and 30 lines of code, and 12% is in methods between 31 and 60 lines of code. The Jenkins codebase is not perfect. It has severe unit size violations: 6% of the codebase is in very long units (more than 60 lines of code).

The second chart in Figure 1-1 shows the quality profile of a 2-star system. Notice that over one-third of the codebase is in units that are over 60 lines of code. Doing maintenance on this system is a very painstaking job.

Finally, the third chart in Figure 1-1 shows the unit size cutoff points for 4 stars. Compare this chart to the first one. You can tell that Jenkins complies to the unit size guideline for 4 stars (although not for 5 stars), since the percentages of code in each category are lower than the 4-star cutoffs.

In a sidebar at the end of each guideline chapter, we present the quality profile categories for that guideline as we use them at SIG to rate maintainability. Specifically, for each guideline, we present the cutoff points and the maximum percentage of code in each category for a rating of 4 stars or higher (top 35% of the benchmark).

1.6 An Overview of the Maintainability Guidelines

In the following chapters, we will present the guidelines one by one, but here we list all 10 guidelines together to give you a quick overview. We advise you to read this book starting with Chapter 2 and work your way through sequentially.

Write short units of code (Chapter 2)
> Shorter units (that is, methods and constructors) are easier to analyze, test, and reuse.

Write simple units of code (Chapter 3)
> Units with fewer decision points are easier to analyze and test.

Write code once (Chapter 4)
> Duplication of source code should be avoided at all times, since changes will need to be made in each copy. Duplication is also a source of regression bugs.

Keep unit interfaces small (Chapter 5)
> Units (methods and constructors) with fewer parameters are easier to test and reuse.

Separate concerns in modules (Chapter 6)
> Modules (classes) that are loosely coupled are easier to modify and lead to a more modular system.

Couple architecture components loosely (Chapter 7)
> Top-level components of a system that are more loosely coupled are easier to modify and lead to a more modular system.

Keep architecture components balanced (Chapter 8)
> A well-balanced architecture, with not too many and not too few components, of uniform size, is the most modular and enables easy modification through separation of concerns.

Keep your codebase small (Chapter 9)
> A large system is difficult to maintain, because more code needs to be analyzed, changed, and tested. Also, maintenance productivity *per line of code* is lower in a large system than in a small system.

Automate development pipeline and tests (Chapter 10)

> Automated tests (that is, tests that can be executed without manual intervention) enable near-instantaneous feedback on the effectiveness of modifications. Manual tests do not scale.

Write clean code (Chapter 11)

> Having irrelevant artifacts such as TODOs and dead code in your codebase makes it more difficult for new team members to become productive. Therefore, it makes maintenance less efficient.

Write Short Units of Code

Any fool can write code that a computer can understand. Good programmers write code that humans can understand.

— Martin Fowler

Guideline:

- **Limit the length of code units to 15 lines of code**.
- Do this by **not writing units that are longer than 15 lines of code** in the first place, or by **splitting long units into multiple smaller units** until each unit has at most 15 lines of code.
- This improves maintainability because **small units are easy to understand, easy to test, and easy to reuse**.

Units are the smallest groups of code that can be maintained and executed independently. In C#, units are methods or constructors. A unit is always executed as a whole. It is not possible to invoke just a few lines of a unit. Therefore, the smallest piece of code that can be reused and tested is a unit.

Consider the code snippet presented next. Given a customer identifier in a URL, this code generates a list of all of the customer's bank accounts along with the balance of each account. The list is returned as a string formatted according to the JSON standard, and also includes the overall total balance. It checks the validity of the bank account numbers using a checksum and skips invalid numbers. See the sidebar "The 11-Check for Bank Account Numbers" on page 12 for an explanation of the checksum used.

The 11-Check for Bank Account Numbers

The 11-check is a checksum used to validate Dutch nine-digit bank account numbers. The checksum is a weighted sum of the nine digits of an account number. The weights are the position of the digit in the bank account number, from right to left. The leftmost digit has weight 9, while the rightmost digit has weight 1. A bank account number is valid if and only if this checksum is an integer multiple of 11. This checksum can detect mistakes in which one digit of a bank number is wrong.

As an example, consider bank account number **12.34.56.789**. With the bank account numbers in bold, let us count its sum from left to right: $(\mathbf{1} \times 9) + (\mathbf{2} \times 8) + (\mathbf{3} \times 7) + (\mathbf{4} \times 6) + (\mathbf{5} \times 5) + (\mathbf{6} \times 4) + (\mathbf{7} \times 3) + (\mathbf{8} \times 2) + (\mathbf{9} \times 1) = 165$. Its checksum is therefore valid, because $165 = 15 \times 11$.

```csharp
public void DoGet(HttpRequest req, HttpResponse resp)
{
    resp.ContentType = "application/json";
    string command = "SELECT account, balance " +
        "FROM ACCTS WHERE id=" + req.Params[
            ConfigurationManager.AppSettings["request.parametername"]];
    SqlDataAdapter dataAdapter = new SqlDataAdapter(command,
        ConfigurationManager.AppSettings["handler.serverstring"]);
    DataSet dataSet = new DataSet();
    dataAdapter.Fill(dataSet, "ACCTS");
    DataTable dataTable = dataSet.Tables[0];
    try
    {
        float totalBalance = 0;
        int rowNum = 0;
        resp.Write("{\"balances\":[");
        while (dataTable.Rows.GetEnumerator().MoveNext())
        {
            rowNum++;
            DataRow results = (DataRow)dataTable.Rows.GetEnumerator().Current;
            // Assuming result is 9-digit bank account number,
            // validate with 11-test:
            int sum = 0;
            for (int i = 0; i < ((string)results["account"]).Length; i++)
            {
                sum = sum + (9 - i) *
                    (int)Char.GetNumericValue(((string)results["account"])[i]);
            }
            if (sum % 11 == 0)
            {
                totalBalance += (float)results["balance"];
                resp.Write($"{{\"{results["account"]}\":{results["balance"]}}}");
            }
            if (rowNum == dataTable.Rows.Count)
```

```
        {
            resp.Write("],\n");
        }
        else
        {
            resp.Write(",");
        }
    }
    resp.Write($"\"total\":{totalBalance}}}\n");
}
catch (SqlException e)
{
    Console.WriteLine($"SQL exception: {e.Message}");
}
}
```

Understanding this unit requires you to keep track of a large number of details. First, there is the ADO.NET connection. Then the checksum is validated in a for loop inside the while loop, which iterates over all records returned by the SQL query. There are also the details of JSON formatting, and the details of handling HTTP requests and responses, to keep in mind.

The for loop in the middle of the unit implements the checksum validation. While conceptually not that difficult, this type of code requires testing. That is easier said than done, since you can only test the code by invoking the DoGet method. That requires first creating HttpRequest and HttpResponse objects. It also requires making a database server available and populating it with account numbers to test. After the call to DoGet, all you have is a JSON-formatted string hidden in the HttpResponse object. To test whether the total balance is correct, you have to extract this value from the JSON-formatted string.

The checksum code is also hard to reuse. The only way to execute the checksum code is to call DoGet. Consequently, any future code that wants to reuse the checksum code needs to have a SQL database available just to provide the bank account number to check.

Long units tend to be hard to test, reuse, and understand. In the example just given, the root cause is that DoGet is mixing (at least) four responsibilities: handling an HTTP GET request, accessing data from a database, executing some business logic, and transferring the result to the data transfer format of choice—in this case, JSON. Together, DoGet has 46 lines of code. A shorter unit would simply not accommodate that many responsibilities.

Every line that is not empty and does not contain only a comment counts as a line of code. When counting the length of a unit, we start at the line containing the first opening brace.

2.1 Motivation

The advantages of short units are that they are easy to test, easy to analyze, and easy to reuse.

Short Units Are Easy to Test

Units encapsulate the application logic of your system, and typically much testing effort is spent on validating the application logic's correctness. This is because the C# compiler will not detect errors in the application logic automatically, and neither will your editor or IDE (integrated development environment; e.g., Visual Studio). Code with a single responsibility is easier to test. In general, short units may do only one thing, while long units do multiple things and tend to have more responsibilities. A unit with one responsibility is easier to test, since it implements a single indivisible task. That allows the test to be isolated (specific to the unit) and simple. Chapter 10 discusses testing in more detail.

Short Units Are Easy to Analyze

It takes less time to read all the code in a short unit in order to analyze how the unit works internally than it does in a long unit. This may not be apparent when you are writing new code, but it makes all the difference when you are modifying existing code. This is not an exceptional situation, since maintenance begins the day after the project is started.

Short Units Are Easy to Reuse

A unit should always be invoked in at least one method (otherwise, the unit is dead code). In a system, you can reuse a unit by invoking it in more than one method. Small units are better candidates for reuse than long units. Long units tend to offer specific details or provide a specific combination of functionalities. As a result, they have more specialized functionality than short units. This makes reuse hard, because it is not very likely that the specific functionality of a long unit is suitable. In contrast, short units tend to be more generic. This makes reuse easier, because it is more likely to fit your needs. Reusing code also helps keep the total code volume low (see Chapter 9).

 Copying and pasting a unit is *not* what we mean when we speak about reuse. That type of reuse leads to duplication, which is to be avoided at all times (see Chapter 4).

2.2 How to Apply the Guideline

Following this guideline is not difficult when you know the right techniques, but it requires discipline. This section presents two techniques that we find particularly important. When writing a new unit, never let it grow beyond 15 lines of code. That means that well before you reach 15 lines of code, you need to start thinking about how to add further functionality. Does it *really* belong in the unit you are writing, or should it go into its own unit? When a unit grows beyond 15 lines of code despite your efforts, you need to shorten it.

When Writing a New Unit

Assume you are writing a class that represents a level in CsPacMan, the codebase we use for a number of examples in this book. See the sidebar "About CsPacMan" on page 16 for an introduction to it. This class provides public Start and Stop methods that are called from buttons in the user interface of the game. A level maintains a list of *observers*: classes that need to be informed whenever the level has finished.

The most basic version of the Start method checks whether the game is already in progress. If so, it silently returns; otherwise, it updates inProgress, a private member to keep track of its state:

```
public void Start()
{
    if (inProgress)
    {
        return;
    }
    inProgress = true;
}
```

So far our unit contains only seven lines of code. At this point, we can add a unit test for our unit. When you use TDD (test-driven development), you already have a unit test at this point. Unit testing is discussed in Chapter 10.

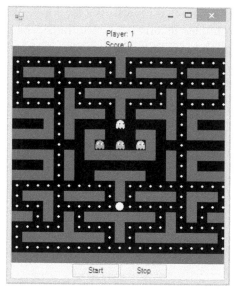
When Extending a Unit with New Functionality

When you extend your system with new functionality, you will see that units start to grow longer. Discipline is required to adhere to a strict size limit. The next thing the `Start` method needs is functionality that updates all observers of the level to inform them about the current state. Here is how that works if we add code that tells all observers the level has been lost if the player has died, and that tells all observers that the level is won if any pellets are left:

```
public void Start()
{
    if (inProgress)
```

```
    {
        return;
    }
    inProgress = true;
    // Update observers if player died:
    if (!IsAnyPlayerAlive())
    {
        foreach (LevelObserver o in observers)
        {
            o.LevelLost();
        }
    }
    // Update observers if all pellets eaten:
    if (RemainingPellets() == 0)
    {
        foreach (LevelObserver o in observers)
        {
            o.LevelWon();
        }
    }
}
```

Adding the code to update observers made our unit grow to 21 lines of code (and 23 lines in total, including the 2 lines that contain comments). After testing the behavior of this new code, you are probably already thinking about the next functionality to implement. However, you need to refactor first to follow the guideline of this chapter.

Using Refactoring Techniques to Apply the Guideline

This section discusses two refactoring techniques to apply the guideline and achieve shorter units of code.

Refactoring technique: Extract Method

One refactoring technique that works in this case is Extract Method. In the following snippet, this technique is applied to extract a method from the former snippet:

```
public void Start()
{
    if (inProgress)
    {
        return;
    }
    inProgress = true;
    UpdateObservers();
}

private void UpdateObservers()
{
    // Update observers if player died:
    if (!IsAnyPlayerAlive())
```

```
    {
        foreach (LevelObserver o in observers)
        {
            o.LevelLost();
        }
    }
    // Update observers if all pellets eaten:
    if (RemainingPellets() == 0)
    {
        foreach (LevelObserver o in observers)
        {
            o.LevelWon();
        }
    }
}
```

As you can see, the unit (the method called `Start`) that had grown to 21 lines of code is now back to 8 lines of code, well below the limit of 15 lines. A new unit (method), called `UpdateObservers`, has been added. However, this method itself has 16 lines of code, which is not under the limit of 15 lines (we will fix this in a moment). There is an additional benefit. Starting or resuming a level is not the only place where observers need to be updated; they also need to be informed after every move (of the player or any of the ghosts). Implementing that is easy now: just call `UpdateObservers` from `Move`, the method that controls the movement of the player and all ghosts.

The new method still has two responsibilities, as indicated by the comments. We have to refactor the code further, applying Extract Method two more times:

```
public void UpdateObservers()
{
    UpdateObserversPlayerDied();
    UpdateObserversPelletsEaten();
}

private void UpdateObserversPlayerDied()
{
    if (!IsAnyPlayerAlive())
    {
        foreach (LevelObserver o in observers)
        {
            o.LevelLost();
        }
    }
}

private void UpdateObserversPelletsEaten()
{
    if (RemainingPellets() == 0)
    {
        foreach (LevelObserver o in observers)
        {
```

```
            o.LevelWon();
        }
    }
}
```

There is no need for the comments anymore: they have been replaced by the names of the new methods. Using short units makes source code self-explanatory, as the names of the methods take over the role of comments. There is a price, however: the total number of code lines has increased, from 16 to 25.

Writing maintainable code is always a trade-off between different guidelines. When splitting a unit into multiple units, you might increase the total number of code lines. That seems to contradict the guideline of keeping the codebase small (see Chapter 9). However, you have decreased the length and complexity of units that need to be tested and understood. Therefore, maintainability has improved. While keeping the codebase small is a good practice, the advantages of short units far outweigh the increase in overall volume—especially given the marginal volume increase in this case.

That writing maintainable code is always a trade-off is also evident in the choices made by the JPacman authors. In the source code as it appears on GitHub, Extract Method has been applied once, resulting in the 16-line version of UpdateObservers. The authors of JPacman have not chosen to split UpdateObservers into UpdateObserversPlayerDied and UpdateObserversPelletsEaten.

Refactoring technique: Replace Method with Method Object

In this example, it was easy to apply the Extract Method refactoring technique. The reason is that the groups of code lines that were extracted did not access any local variables, nor did they return any value. Sometimes, you want to extract a method that *does* access local variables. It is always possible to pass local variables as parameters to the extracted method. However, this may lead to long parameter lists, which are a problem in themselves (see Chapter 5). Return values can be even more troublesome, as in C# you can return only a single value from a method. In these cases, you can use a second refactoring technique, called *Replace Method with Method Object*.

JPacman contains a snippet for which this refactoring is applicable. Consider the following 21-line method from the class BoardFactory:

```
public Board CreateBoard(Square[,] grid)
{
    Debug.Assert(grid != null);

    Board board = new Board(grid);

    int width = board.Width;
    int height = board.Height;
    for (int x = 0; x < width; x++)
```

```
    {
        for (int y = 0; y < height; y++)
        {
            Square square = grid[x, y];
            foreach (Direction dir in Direction.Values)
            {
                int dirX = (width + x + dir.DeltaX) % width;
                int dirY = (height + y + dir.DeltaY) % height;
                Square neighbour = grid[dirX, dirY];
                square.Link(neighbour, dir);
            }
        }
    }

    return board;
}
```

The four lines inside the innermost for loop are a candidate for the Extract Method technique. However, together these four lines use six local variables—width, height, x, y, dir, and square—and one pseudovariable, the grid parameter. If you apply the Extract Method technique, you will have to pass seven parameters to the extracted method:

```
private void SetLink(Square square, Direction dir, int x, int y,
    int width, int height, Square[,] grid)
{
    int dirX = (width + x + dir.DeltaX) % width;
    int dirY = (height + y + dir.DeltaY) % height;
    Square neighbour = grid[dirX, dirY];
    square.Link(neighbour, dir);
}
```

The refactored CreateBoard method would look like this:

```
public Board CreateBoard(Square[,] grid)
{
    Debug.Assert(grid != null);

    Board board = new Board(grid);

    int width = board.Width;
    int height = board.Height;
    for (int x = 0; x < width; x++)
    {
        for (int y = 0; y < height; y++)
        {
            Square square = grid[x, y];
            foreach (Direction dir in Direction.Values)
            {
                SetLink(square, dir, x, y, width, height, grid);
            }
        }
    }
```

```
    }

    return board;
}
```

Let us try the Replace Method with Method Object technique instead. In this technique, we create a new class that will take over the role of CreateBoard, the method we are refactoring:

```
internal class BoardCreator
{
    private Square[,] grid;
    private Board board;
    private int width;
    private int height;

    internal BoardCreator(Square[,] grid)
    {
        Debug.Assert(grid != null);
        this.grid = grid;
        this.board = new Board(grid);
        this.width = board.Width;
        this.height = board.Height;
    }

    internal Board Create()
    {
        for (int x = 0; x < width; x++)
        {
            for (int y = 0; y < height; y++)
            {
                Square square = grid[x, y];
                foreach (Direction dir in Direction.Values)
                {
                    SetLink(square, dir, x, y);
                }
            }
        }
        return this.board;
    }

    private void SetLink(Square square, Direction dir, int x, int y)
    {
        int dirX = (width + x + dir.DeltaX) % width;
        int dirY = (height + y + dir.DeltaY) % height;
        Square neighbour = grid[dirX, dirY];
        square.Link(neighbour, dir);
    }
}
```

In this new class, three local variables (board, width, and height) and one parameter (grid) of the CreateBoard method have been turned into (private) fields of the new class. These fields are accessible to all methods of the new class. Hence, they no longer need to be passed around as parameters. The four lines of the innermost for loop now appear in a new method, SetLink, that has four parameters, not seven.

We're almost done. To complete the refactoring, we have to change the original Crea teBoard method as follows:

```
public Board CreateBoard(Square[,] grid)
{
    return new BoardCreator(grid).Create();
}
```

Not only have we ended up only with methods shorter than 15 lines of code and avoided creating methods with long parameter lists, but the code is actually easier to read, test, and reuse.

2.3 Common Objections to Writing Short Units

While writing short units may *sound* simple, software developers often find it quite difficult in practice. The following are typical objections to the principle explained in this chapter.

Objection: Having More Units Is Bad for Performance

"Writing short units means having more units, and therefore more method calls. That will never perform."

Indeed, theoretically, there is a performance penalty for having more units. There will be more method invocations (compared to having fewer, longer units). For each invocation, a bit of work needs to be done by the .Net runtime. In practice, this is almost never a problem. In the worst case, we are talking about microseconds. Unless a unit is executed hundreds of thousands of times in a loop, the performance penalty of a method invocation is not noticeable. Also, the C# compiler is *very* good at optimizing the overhead of method invocations.

Except for very specific cases in enterprise software development, you can focus on maintainability without sacrificing performance. An example is when a method is invoked hundreds of thousands of times in the case of certain algorithms. This is probably one of the very few cases in a programmer's life where you can have your cake and eat it too. We are not saying that there are no performance issues in enterprise software development; however, they seldom, if ever, are caused by excessive method calling.

Do not sacrifice maintainability to optimize for performance, unless solid performance tests have proven that you actually have a performance problem and your performance optimization actually makes a difference.

Objection: Code Is Harder to Read When Spread Out

"Code becomes harder to read when spread out over multiple units."

Well, psychology says that is not the case. People have a working memory of about seven items, so someone who is reading a unit that is significantly longer than seven lines of code cannot process all of it. The exception is probably the original author of a piece of source code while he or she is working on it (but not a week later).

Write code that is easy to read and understand for your successors (and for your future self).

Guideline Encourages Improper Formatting

"Your guideline encourages improper source code formatting."

Do not try to comply with guideline by cutting corners in the area of formatting. We are talking about putting multiple statements or multiple curly brackets on one line. It makes the code slightly harder to read and thus decreases its maintainability. Resist the temptation to do so.

Consider what purpose the guideline really serves. We simply cannot leave unit length unconstrained. That would be akin to removing speed limits in traffic because they discourage being on time. It is perfectly possible to obey speed limits and arrive on time: just leave home a bit earlier. It is equally possible to write short units. Our experience is that 15 lines of properly formatted code is enough to write useful units.

As proof, Table 2-1 presents some data from a typical Java 2 Enterprise Edition system, consisting of Java source files but also some XSD and XSLT. The system, currently in production at a SIG client, provides reporting functionality for its owner. The Java part consists of about 28,000 lines of code (a medium-sized system). Of these 28,000 lines of code, just over 17,000 lines are in units. There are just over 3,000 units in this codebase.

Table 2-1. Distribution of unit length in a real-world enterprise system

Unit length	Number of units (absolute)	Number of units (relative)	Number of lines (absolute)	Number of lines (relative)
1-15	3,071	95.4%	14,032	81.3%
16 or more	149	4.6%	3,221	18.7%
Total	**3,220**	**100%**	**17,253**	**100%**

Out of the 3,220 units in this system, 3,071 (95.4%) are at most 15 lines of code, while 149 units (4.6% of all units) are longer. This shows that it is very possible in practice to write short units—at least for a vast majority of units.

Agree on formatting conventions in your team. Keep units short *and* comply with these conventions.

This Unit Is Impossible to Split Up

"My unit really cannot be split up."

Sometimes, splitting a method is indeed difficult. Take, for instance, a properly formatted `switch` statement in C#. For each case of the `switch` statement, there is a line for the case itself, at least one line to do anything useful, and a line for the `break` statement. So, anything beyond four cases becomes very hard to fit into 15 lines of code, and a `case` statement cannot be split. In Chapter 3, we present some guidelines on how to deal specifically with `switch` statements.

However, it is true that sometimes a source code statement simply cannot be split. A typical example in enterprise software is SQL query construction. Consider the following example (adapted from a real-world system analyzed by the authors of this book):

```csharp
public static void PrintDepartmentEmployees(string department)
{
    Query q = new Query();
    foreach (Employee e in q.AddColumn("FamilyName")
        .AddColumn("Initials")
        .AddColumn("GivenName")
        .AddColumn("AddressLine1")
        .AddColumn("ZIPcode")
        .AddColumn("City")
        .AddTable("EMPLOYEES")
        .AddWhere($"EmployeeDep='{department}'")
        .Execute())
    {
        Console.WriteLine($@"<div name='addressDiv'>
```

```
      {e.FamilyName}, {e.Initials}<br />" +
      "{e.AddressLine1}<br />{e.ZipCode}{e.City}</div>");
    }
}
```

This example has 16 lines of code. However, there are just three statements. The second statement contains an expression that spans nine lines. Indeed, you cannot extract just this statement; neither the Extract Method nor the Replace Method with Method Object technique is applicable, at least not directly. However, the nine-line expression starting with `q.AddColumn("FamilyName")` can be extracted into a new method. But before doing that (and seeing the newly created method grow to over 15 lines when the query gets more complex in the future), rethink the architecture. Is it wise to create a SQL query piece by piece as in this snippet? Should the HTML markup really appear here? A templating solution such as ASP or Razor may be more suitable for the job at hand.

So, if you are faced with a unit that seems impossible to refactor, do not ignore it and move on to another programming task, but indeed raise the issue with your team members and team lead.

When a refactoring seems possible but doesn't make sense, rethink the architecture of your system.

There Is No Visible Advantage in Splitting Units

"Putting code in `DoSomethingOne`, `DoSomethingTwo`, `DoSomethingThree` has no benefit over putting the same code all together in one long `DoSomething`."

Actually, it does, provided you choose better names than `DoSomethingOne`, `DoSomethingTwo`, and so on. Each of the shorter units is, on its own, easier to understand than the long `DoSomething`. More importantly, you may not even need to consider all the parts, especially since each of the method names, when chosen carefully, serves as documentation indicating what the unit of code is supposed to do. Moreover, the long `DoSomething` typically will combine multiple tasks. That means that you can only reuse `DoSomething` if you need the exact same combination. Most likely, you can reuse each of `DoSomethingOne`, `DoSomethingTwo`, and so on much more easily.

Put code in short units (at most 15 lines of code) that have carefully chosen names that describe their function.

2.4 See Also

See Chapters 3, 4, and 5 for additional refactoring techniques. For a discussion on how to test methods, see Chapter 10.

How SIG Rates Unit Size

The size (length) of units (methods and constructors in C#) is one of the eight system properties of the SIG/TÜViT Evaluation Criteria for Trusted Product Maintainability. To rate unit size, every unit of the system is categorized in one of four risk categories depending on the number of lines of code it contains. Table 2-2 lists the four risk categories used in the 2015 version of the SIG/TÜViT Evaluation Criteria.

The criteria (rows) in Table 2-2 are conjunctive: a codebase needs to comply with all four of them. For example, if 6.9% of all lines of code are in methods longer than 60 lines, the codebase can still be rated at 4 stars. However, in that case, at most 22.3% – 6.9% = 15.4% of all lines of code can be in methods that are longer than 30 lines but not longer than 60 lines. To the contrary, if a codebase does not have any methods of more than 60 lines of code, at most 22.3% of all lines of code can be in methods that are longer than 30 lines but not longer than 60 lines.

Table 2-2. Minimum thresholds for a 4-star unit size rating (2015 version of the SIG/ TÜViT Evaluation Criteria)

Lines of code in methods with ...	Percentage allowed for 4 stars for unit size
... more than 60 lines of code	At most 6.9%
... more than 30 lines of code	At most 22.3%
... more than 15 lines of code	At most 43.7%
... at most 15 lines of code	At least 56.3%

See the three quality profiles shown in Figure 2-2 as an example:

- Left: an open source system, in this case Jenkins
- Center: an anonymous system in the SIG benchmark that complies with a 4-star rating for unit size
- Right: the cutoff points for achieving 4-star quality for this quality characteristic

Figure 2-2. *Three quality profiles for unit size*

CHAPTER 3

Write Simple Units of Code

Each problem has smaller problems inside.

—Martin Fowler

Guideline:

- **Limit the number of branch points per unit to 4.**
- Do this by **splitting complex units into simpler ones** and avoiding complex units altogether.
- This improves maintainability because keeping the number of branch points low **makes units easier to modify and test**.

Complexity is an often disputed quality characteristic. Code that appears complex to an outsider or novice developer can appear straightforward to a developer that is intimately familiar with it. To a certain extent, what is "complex" is in the eye of the beholder. There is, however, a point where code becomes so complex that modifying it becomes extremely risky and very time-consuming task, let alone testing the modifications afterward. To keep code maintainable, we must put a limit on complexity. Another reason to measure complexity is knowing the minimum number of tests we need to be sufficiently certain that the system acts predictably. Before we can define such a code complexity limit, we must be able to measure complexity.

A common way to objectively assess complexity is to count the number of possible paths through a piece of code. The idea is that the more paths can be distinguished, the more complex a piece of code is. We can determine the number of paths unambiguously by counting the number of *branch points*. A branch point is a statement where execution can take more than one direction depending on a condition. Examples of branch points in C# code are `if` and `switch` statements (a complete list follows later). Branch points can be counted for a complete codebase, a class, a namespace, or a unit. The number of branch points of a unit is equal to the minimum number of paths needed to cover all branches created by all branch points of that unit. This is called *branch coverage*. However, when you consider all paths through a unit from the first line of the unit to a final statement, combinatory effects are possible. The reason is that it *may* matter whether a branch follows another in a particular order. All possible combinations of branches are the *execution paths* of the unit—that is, the maximum number of paths through the unit.

Consider a unit containing two consecutive if statements. Figure 3-1 depicts the control flow of the unit and shows the difference between branch coverage and execution path coverage.

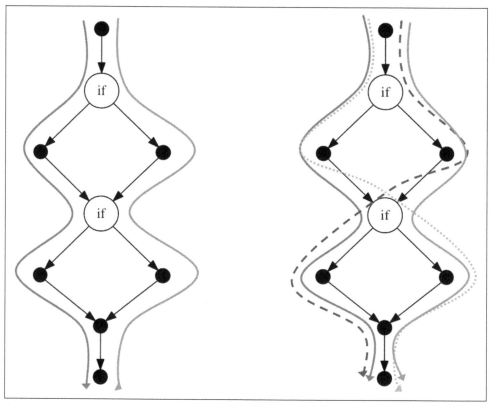

Figure 3-1. Branch coverage and execution path coverage

Suppose the point to the left of the first if statement modifies a database, and the point to the right of the second if statement reads from that database. These are side effects and require us to test the "zigzag" paths as well (the dotted lines in Figure 3-1).

In summary, the number of branch points is the number of paths that cover all branches created by branch points. It is the minimum number of paths and can be zero (for a unit that has no branch points). The number of execution paths is a maximum, and can be very large due to combinatorial explosion. Which one to choose?

The answer is to take the number of branch points plus one. This is called *cyclomatic complexity* or *McCabe complexity*. Consequently, the guideline "limit the number of branch points per unit to 4" is equal to "limit code McCabe complexity to 5." This is the minimum number of test cases that you need to cover a unit such that every path has a part not covered by the other paths. The cyclomatic (McCabe) complexity of a unit is at least one, which is easy to understand as follows. Consider a unit with no branch points. According to the definition, its cyclomatic complexity is one (number of branch points plus one). It also fits intuitively: a unit with no branch points has one execution path, and needs at least one test.

For the sake of completeness: only for units with one exit point, the cyclomatic or McCabe complexity is equal to the number of branch points plus one. It becomes more complex for units with more than one exit point. Do not worry about that: focus on limiting the number of branch points to four.

 The minimum number of tests needed to cover all independent execution paths of a unit is equal to the number of branch points plus one.

Now consider the following example. Given a nationality, the `GetFlagColors` method returns the correct flag colors:

```
public IList<Color> GetFlagColors(Nationality nationality)
{
    List<Color> result;
    switch (nationality)
    {
        case Nationality.DUTCH:
            result = new List<Color> { Color.Red, Color.White, Color.Blue };
            break;
        case Nationality.GERMAN:
            result = new List<Color> { Color.Black, Color.Red, Color.Yellow };
            break;
        case Nationality.BELGIAN:
            result = new List<Color> { Color.Black, Color.Yellow, Color.Red };
            break;
        case Nationality.FRENCH:
            result = new List<Color> { Color.Blue, Color.White, Color.Red };
            break;
        case Nationality.ITALIAN:
            result = new List<Color> { Color.Green, Color.White, Color.Red };
```

```
            break;
        case Nationality.UNCLASSIFIED:
        default:
            result = new List<Color> { Color.Gray };
            break;
    }
    return result;
}
```

The `switch` statement in the method body needs to handle all cases of the nationality enumeration type and return the correct flag colors. As there are five possible nationalities and the unclassified/default case, the number of isolated paths to be tested (control flow branches) is six.

On first sight, the `GetFlagColors` method might seem harmless. Indeed, the method is quite readable, and its behavior is as expected. Still, if we want to test the behavior of this method, we would need six unique test cases (one for each nationality plus one for the default/unclassified case). Writing automated tests might seem excessive for the `GetFlagColors` method, but suppose a developer adds the flag of Luxembourg (which is very similar to the Dutch flag) as a quick fix:

```
...
        case Nationality.DUTCH:
            result = new List<Color> { Color.Red, Color.White, Color.Blue };
        case Nationality.LUXEMBOURGER:
            result = new List<Color> { Color.Red, Color.White, Color.LightBlue };
            break;
        case Nationality.GERMAN:
....
```

Being in a hurry, the developer copied the constructor call for the Dutch flag and updated the last argument to the right color. Unfortunately, the `break` statement escaped the developer's attention, and now all Dutch nationalities will see the flag from Luxembourg on their profile page!

This example looks like a forged scenario, but we know from our consultancy practice that this is what happens to complex code in reality. These types of simple mistakes are also responsible for many "trivial" bugs that could be easily prevented.

To understand why complex code is such a problem for maintenance, it is important to realize that code that starts out quite straightforward tends to grow much more complex over time. Consider the following snippet taken from the codebase of the open source build server Jenkins. There are 20 control flow branches in this code snippet. Imagine having to modify or test this method:

```
/**
 * Retrieve a user by its ID, and create a new one if requested.
 * @return
 *      An existing or created user. May be {@code null} if a user does not exis
 *      and {@code create} is false.
```

```
*/
private static User getOrCreate(string id, string fullName, bool create)
{
    string idkey = idStrategy().keyFor(id);

    byNameLock.readLock().doLock();
    User u;
    try
    {
        u = byName.get(idkey);
    }
    finally
    {
        byNameLock.readLock().unlock();
    }
    FileInfo configFile = getConfigFileFor(id);
    if (!configFile.Exists && !Directory.Exists(configFile.Directory.FullName))
    {
        // check for legacy users and migrate if safe to do so.
        FileInfo[] legacy = getLegacyConfigFilesFor(id);
        if (legacy != null && legacy.Length > 0)
        {
            foreach (FileInfo legacyUserDir in legacy)
            {
                XmlFile legacyXml = new XmlFile(XmlFile.XSTREAM,
                                new FileInfo(Path.Combine(
                                legacyUserDir.FullName, "config.xml")));
                try
                {
                    object o = legacyXml.read();
                    if (o is User)
                    {
                        if (idStrategy().equals(id, legacyUserDir.Name)
                            && !idStrategy()
                            .filenameOf(legacyUserDir.Name)
                            .Equals(legacyUserDir.Name))
                        {
                            try
                            {
                                File.Move(legacyUserDir.FullName,
                                    configFile.Directory.FullName);
                            }
                            catch (IOException)
                            {
                                LOGGER.log(Level.WARNING,
                                    "Failed to migrate user record from {0} " +
                                    "to {1}", new Object[] {legacyUserDir,
                                        configFile.Directory.FullName
                                    });
                            }
                            break;
                        }
```

```
                }
                else
                {
                    LOGGER.log(Level.FINE,
                        "Unexpected object loaded from {0}: {1}",
                        new object[] { legacyUserDir, o });
                }
            }
            catch (IOException e)
            {
                LOGGER.log(Level.FINE,
                    string.Format(
                        "Exception trying to load user from {0}: {1}",
                        new Object[] { legacyUserDir, e.Message }),
                    e);
            }
        }
    }
}
if (u == null && (create || configFile.Exists))
{
    User tmp = new User(id, fullName);
    User prev;
    byNameLock.readLock().doLock();
    try
    {
        prev = byName.putIfAbsent(idkey, u = tmp);
    }
    finally
    {
        byNameLock.readLock().unlock();
    }
    if (prev != null)
    {
        u = prev; // if some has already put a value in the map, use it
        if (LOGGER.isLoggable(Level.FINE)
            && !fullName.Equals(prev.getFullName()))
        {
            LOGGER.log(Level.FINE,
                "mismatch on fullName ('" + fullName + "' vs. '"
                + prev.getFullName() + "') for '" + id + "'",
                new Exception());
        }
    }
    else if (!id.Equals(fullName) && !configFile.Exists)
    {
        // JENKINS-16332: since the fullName may not be recoverable
        // from the id, and various code may store the id only, we
        // must save the fullName
        try
        {
            u.save();
```

```
        }
        catch (IOException x)
        {
            LOGGER.log(Level.WARNING, null, x);
        }
      }
    }
    return u;
}
```

3.1 Motivation

Based on the code examples in the previous section, keeping your units simple is important for two main reasons:

- A simple unit is easier to understand, and thus modify, than a complex one.
- Simple units ease testing.

Simple Units Are Easier to Modify

Units with high complexity are generally hard to understand, which makes them hard to modify. The first code example of the first section was not overly complicated, but it would be when it checks for, say, 15 or more nationalities. The second code example covers many use cases for looking up or creating users. Understanding the second code example in order to make a functional change is quite a challenge. The time it takes to understand the code makes modification harder.

Simple Units Are Easier to Test

There is a good reason you should keep your units simple: to make the process of testing easier. If there are six control flow branches in a unit, you will need at least six test cases to cover all of them. Consider the GetFlagColors method: six tests to cover five nationalities plus the default case would prevent trivial bugs from being introduced by maintenance work.

3.2 How to Apply the Guideline

As explained at the beginning of this chapter, we need to limit the number of branch points to four. In C# the following statements and operators count as branch points:

- if
- case
- ?, ??

- `&&`, `||`
- `while`
- `for`, `foreach`
- `catch`

So how can we limit the number of branch points? Well, this is mainly a matter of identifying the proper causes of high complexity. In a lot of cases, a complex unit consists of several code blocks glued together, where the complexity of the unit is the sum of its parts. In other cases, the complexity arises as the result of nested `if-then-else` statements, making the code increasingly harder to understand with each level of nesting. Another possibility is the presence of a long chain of `if-then-else` statements or a long `switch` statement, of which the `GetFlagColors` method in the introduction is an example.

Each of these cases has its own problem, and thus, its own solution. The first case, where a unit consists of several code blocks that execute almost independently, is a good candidate for refactoring using the *Extract Method* pattern. This way of reducing complexity is similar to Chapter 2. But what to do when faced with the other cases of complexity?

Dealing with Conditional Chains

A chain of `if-then-else` statements has to make a decision every time a conditional `if` is encountered. An easy-to-handle situation is the one in which the conditionals are mutually exclusive; that is, they each apply to a different situation. This is also the typical use case for a `switch` statement, like the switch from the `GetFlagColors` method.

There are many ways to simplify this type of complexity, and selecting the best solution is a trade-off that depends on the specific situation. For the `GetFlagColors` method we present two alternatives to reduce complexity. The first is the introduction of a `Map` data structure that maps nationalities to specific `Flag` objects. This refactoring reduces the complexity of the `GetFlagColors` method from McCabe 7 to McCabe 2.

```
private static Dictionary<Nationality, IList<Color>> FLAGS =
    new Dictionary<Nationality, IList<Color>>();

static FlagFactoryWithMap()
{
    FLAGS[Nationality.DUTCH] = new List<Color>{ Color.Red, Color.White,
        Color.Blue };
    FLAGS[Nationality.GERMAN] = new List<Color>{ Color.Black, Color.Red,
        Color.Yellow };
    FLAGS[Nationality.BELGIAN] = new List<Color>{ Color.Black, Color.Yellow,
```

```
            Color.Red };
        FLAGS[Nationality.FRENCH] = new List<Color>{ Color.Blue, Color.White,
            Color.Red };
        FLAGS[Nationality.ITALIAN] = new List<Color>{ Color.Green, Color.White,
            Color.Red };
    }

    public IList<Color> GetFlagColors(Nationality nationality)
    {
        IList<Color> colors = FLAGS[nationality];
        return colors ?? new List<Color> { Color.Gray };
    }
```

A second, more advanced way to reduce the complexity of the `GetFlagColors` method is to apply a refactoring pattern that separates functionality for different flags in different flag types. You can do this by applying the *Replace Conditional with Polymorphism* pattern: each flag will get its own type that implements a general interface. The polymorphic behavior of the C# language will ensure that the right functionality is called during runtime.

For this refactoring, we start with a general `IFlag` interface:

```
public interface IFlag
{
    IList<Color> Colors { get; }
}
```

and specific flag types for different nationalities, such as for the Dutch:

```
public class DutchFlag : IFlag
{
    public IList<Color> Colors
    {
        get
        {
            return new List<Color> { Color.Red, Color.White, Color.Blue };
        }
    }
}
```

and the Italian:

```
public class ItalianFlag : IFlag
{
    public IList<Color> Colors
    {
        get
        {
            return new List<Color> { Color.Green, Color.White, Color.Red };
        }
    }
}
```

The `GetFlagColors` method now becomes even more concise and less error-prone:

```csharp
private static readonly Dictionary<Nationality, IFlag> FLAGS =
    new Dictionary<Nationality, IFlag>();

static FlagFactory()
{
    FLAGS[Nationality.DUTCH] = new DutchFlag();
    FLAGS[Nationality.GERMAN] = new GermanFlag();
    FLAGS[Nationality.BELGIAN] = new BelgianFlag();
    FLAGS[Nationality.FRENCH] = new FrenchFlag();
    FLAGS[Nationality.ITALIAN] = new ItalianFlag();
}

public IList<Color> GetFlagColors(Nationality nationality)
{
    IFlag flag = FLAGS[nationality];
    flag = flag ?? new DefaultFlag();
    return flag.Colors;
}
```

This refactoring offers the most flexible implementation. For example, it allows the flag type hierarchy to grow over time by implementing new flag types and testing these types in isolation. A drawback of this refactoring is that it introduces more code spread out over more classes. The developer much choose between extensibility and conciseness.

Dealing with Nesting

Suppose a unit has a deeply nested conditional, as in the following example. Given a binary search tree root node and an integer, the `CalculateDepth` method determines whether the integer occurs in the tree. If so, the method returns the depth of the integer in the tree; otherwise, it throws a `TreeException`:

```csharp
public static int CalculateDepth(BinaryTreeNode<int> t, int n)
{
    int depth = 0;
    if (t.Value == n)
    {
        return depth;
    }
    else
    {
        if (n < t.Value)
        {
            BinaryTreeNode<int> left = t.Left;
            if (left == null)
            {
                throw new TreeException("Value not found in tree!");
            }
            else
```

```
        {
            return 1 + CalculateDepth(left, n);
        }
    }
    else
    {
        BinaryTreeNode<int> right = t.Right;
        if (right == null)
        {
            throw new TreeException("Value not found in tree!");
        }
        else
        {
            return 1 + CalculateDepth(right, n);
        }
    }
}
}
```

To improve readability, we can get rid of the nested conditional by identifying the distinct cases and insert `return` statements for these. In terms of refactoring, this is called the *Replace Nested Conditional with Guard Clauses* pattern. The result will be the following method:

```
public static int CalculateDepth(BinaryTreeNode<int> t, int n)
{
    int depth = 0;
    if (t.Value == n)
    {
        return depth;
    }
    if ((n < t.Value) && (t.Left != null))
    {
        return 1 + CalculateDepth(t.Left, n);
    }
    if ((n > t.Value) && (t.Right != null))
    {
        return 1 + CalculateDepth(t.Right, n);
    }
    throw new TreeException("Value not found in tree!");
}
```

Although the unit is now easier to understand, its complexity has not decreased. In order to reduce the complexity, you should extract the nested conditionals to separate methods. The result will be as follows:

```
public static int CalculateDepth(BinaryTreeNode<int> t, int n)
{
    int depth = 0;
    if (t.Value == n)
    {
        return depth;
```

```
        }
        else
        {
            return TraverseByValue(t, n);
        }
    }

    private static int TraverseByValue(BinaryTreeNode<int> t, int n)
    {
        BinaryTreeNode<int> childNode = GetChildNode(t, n);
        if (childNode == null)
        {
            throw new TreeException("Value not found in tree!");
        }
        else
        {
            return 1 + CalculateDepth(childNode, n);
        }
    }

    private static BinaryTreeNode<int> GetChildNode(
        BinaryTreeNode<int> t, int n)
    {
        if (n < t.Value)
        {
            return t.Left;
        }
        else
        {
            return t.Right;
        }
    }
}
```

This actually *does* decrease the complexity of the unit. Now we have achieved two things: the methods are easier to understand, and they are easier to test in isolation since we can now write unit tests for the distinct functionalities.

3.3 Common Objections to Writing Simple Units of Code

Of course, when you are writing code, units can easily become complex. You may argue that high complexity is bound to arise or that reducing unit complexity in your codebase will not help to increase the maintainability of your system. Such objections are discussed next.

Objection: High Complexity Cannot Be Avoided

"Our domain is very complex, and therefore high code complexity is unavoidable."

When you are working in a complex domain—such as optimizing logistical problems, real-time visualizations, or anything that demands advanced application logic—

it is natural to think that the domain's complexity carries over to the implementation, and that this is an unavoidable fact of life.

We argue against this common interpretation. Complexity in the domain does not require the technical implementation to be complex as well. In fact, it is your responsibility as a developer to simplify problems such that they lead to simple code. Even if the system as a whole performs complex functionality, it does not mean that units on the lowest level should be complex as well. In cases where a system needs to process many conditions and exceptions (such as certain legislative requirements), one solution may be to implement a default, simple process and model the exceptions explicitly.

It is true that the more demanding a domain is, the more effort the developer must expend to build technically simple solutions. But it can be done! We have seen many highly maintainable systems solving complex business problems. In fact, we believe that the only way to solve complex business problems and keep them under control is through simple code.

Objection: Splitting Up Methods Does Not Reduce Complexity

"Replacing one method with McCabe 15 by three methods with McCabe 5 each means that overall McCabe is still 15 (and therefore, there are 15 control flow branches overall). So nothing is gained."

Of course, you will not decrease the overall McCabe complexity of a system by refactoring a method into several new methods. But from a maintainability perspective, there is an advantage to doing so: it will become easier to test and understand the code that was written. So, as we already mentioned, newly written unit tests allow you to more easily identify the root cause of your failing tests.

 Put your code in simple units (at most four branch points) that have carefully chosen names describing their function and cases.

3.4 See Also

See also Chapter 2 on refactoring patterns for splitting units up in smaller units.

How SIG Rates Unit Complexity

The complexity (McCabe) of units (methods and constructors in C#) is one of the eight system properties of the SIG/TÜViT Evaluation Criteria for Trusted Product Maintainability. To rate unit complexity, every unit of the system is categorized in one of four risk categories depending on its McCabe measurement. Table 3-1 lists the four risk categories used in the 2015 version of the SIG/TÜViT Evaluation Criteria.

The criteria (rows) in Table 3-1 are conjunctive: a codebase needs to comply with all four of them. For example, if 1.5% of all lines of code are in methods with a McCabe over 25, it can still be rated at 4 stars. However, in that case, at most 10.0% - 1.5% = 8.5% of all lines of code can be in methods that have a McCabe over 10 but not over 25.

Table 3-1. Minimum thresholds for a 4-star unit complexity rating (2015 version of the SIG/TÜViT Evaluation Criteria)

Lines of code in methods with ...	Percentage allowed for 4 stars for unit complexity
... a McCabe above 25	At most 1.5%
... a McCabe above 10	At most 10.0%
... a McCabe above 5	At most 25.2%
... a McCabe of at most 5	At least 74.8%

See the three quality profiles in Figure 3-2 as an example:

- Left: an open source system, in this case Jenkins
- Center: an anonymous system in the SIG benchmark that complies with a 4-star rating for unit complexity
- Right: the cutoff points for achieving 4-star quality for this quality characteristic

Figure 3-2. Three quality profiles for unit complexity

CHAPTER 4

Write Code Once

Number one in the stink parade is duplicated code.

—Kent Beck and Martin Fowler,
Bad Smells in Code

Guideline:

- **Do not copy code.**
- Do this by **writing reusable, generic code and/or calling existing methods instead.**
- This improves maintainability because **when code is copied, bugs need to be fixed at multiple places**, which is inefficient and error-prone.

Copying existing code looks like a quick win—why write something anew when it already exists? The point is: copied code leads to duplicates, and duplicates are a problem. As the quote above indicates, some even say that duplicates are the biggest software quality problem of all.

Consider a system that manages bank accounts. In this system, money transfers between accounts are represented by objects of the Transfer class (not shown here). The bank offers checking accounts represented by class CheckingAccount:

```
public class CheckingAccount
{
    private int transferLimit = 100;

    public Transfer MakeTransfer(String counterAccount, Money amount)
    {
        // 1. Check withdrawal limit:
```

```
        if (amount.GreaterThan(this.transferLimit))
        {
            throw new BusinessException("Limit exceeded!");
        }
        // 2. Assuming result is 9-digit bank account number, validate 11-test:
        int sum = 0;
        for (int i = 0; i < counterAccount.Length; i++)
        {
            sum = sum + (9 - i) * (int)Char.GetNumericValue(
                counterAccount[i]);
        }
        if (sum % 11 == 0)
        {
            // 3. Look up counter account and make transfer object:
            CheckingAccount acct = Accounts.FindAcctByNumber(counterAccount);
            Transfer result = new Transfer(this, acct, amount);
            return result;
        }
        else
        {
            throw new BusinessException("Invalid account number!");
        }
    }
}
```

Given the account number of the account to transfer money to (as a string), the Make Transfer method creates a Transfer object. MakeTransfer first checks whether the amount to be transferred does not exceed a certain limit. In this example, the limit is simply hardcoded. MakeTransfer then checks whether the number of the account to transfer the money to complies with a checksum (see the sidebar "The 11-Check for Bank Account Numbers" on page 12 for an explanation of the checksum used). If that is the case, the object that represents this account is retrieved, and a Transfer object is created and returned.

Now assume the bank introduces a new account type, called a savings account. A savings account does not have a transfer limit, but it does have a restriction: money can only be transferred to one particular (fixed) checking account. The idea is that the account owner chooses once to couple a particular checking account with a savings account.

A class is needed to represent this new account type. Suppose the existing class is simply copied, renamed, and adapted. This would be the result:

```
public class SavingsAccount
{
    public CheckingAccount RegisteredCounterAccount { get; set; }

    public Transfer makeTransfer(string counterAccount, Money amount)
    {
        // 1. Assuming result is 9-digit bank account number, validate 11-test:
```

```
int sum = 0; ❶
for (int i = 0; i < counterAccount.Length; i++)
{
    sum = sum + (9 - i) * (int)Char.GetNumericValue(
        counterAccount[i]);
}
if (sum % 11 == 0)
{
    // 2. Look up counter account and make transfer object:
    CheckingAccount acct = Accounts.FindAcctByNumber(counterAccount);
    Transfer result = new Transfer(this, acct, amount); ❷
    // 3. Check whether withdrawal is to registered counter account:
    if (result.CounterAccount.Equals(this.RegisteredCounterAccount))
    {
        return result;
    }
    else
    {
        throw new BusinessException("Counter-account not registered!");
    }
}
else
{
    throw new BusinessException("Invalid account number!!");
}
}
}
```

❶ Start of code clone.

❷ End of code clone.

Both classes exist in the same codebase. By copying and pasting an existing class, we have introduced some duplicated code in the codebase. There are now two fragments (ten lines of code each) of consecutive lines of code that are exactly the same. These fragments are called *code clones* or *duplicates*.

Now suppose a bug is discovered in the implementation of the 11-test (the for loop that iterates over the characters in counterAccount). This bug now needs to be fixed in both duplicates. This is additional work, making maintenance less efficient. Moreover, if the fix is only made in one duplicate but the other is overlooked, the bug is only half fixed.

Resist the temptation of gaining a short-term advantage by copying and pasting code. For every future adjustment to either duplicate, you will need to revisit all duplicates.

Coding is about finding *generic* solutions for *specific problems*. Either reuse (by calling) an existing, generic method in your codebase, or make an existing method more generic.

Types of Duplication

We define a *duplicate* or *code clone* as an identical piece of code at least six lines long. The line count excludes whitespace and comments, just like in the regular definition of "line of code" (see also Chapter 1). That means that the lines need to be *exactly* the same to be considered a duplicate. Such clones are called *Type 1 clones*. It does not matter where the duplicates occur. Two clones can be in the same method, in different methods in the same class, or in different methods in different classes in the same codebase. Code clones can cross method boundaries. For instance, if the following fragment appears twice in the codebase, it is considered one clone of six lines of code, not two clones of three lines each:

```
public void SetGivenName(string givenName)
{
    this.givenName = givenName;
}

public void SetFamilyName(string familyName)
{
    this.familyName = familyName;
}
```

The following two methods are not considered duplicates of each other even though they differ only in literals and the names of identifiers:

```
public void SetPageWidthInInches(float newWidth)
{
    float cmPerInch = 2.54f;
    this.pageWidthInCm = newWidth * cmPerInch;
    // A few more lines.
}

public void SetPageWidthInPoints(float newWidth)
{
    float cmPerPoint = 0.0352777f;
    this.pageWidthInCm = newWidth * cmPerPoint;
    // A few more lines (same as in setPageWidthInInches).
}
```

Two fragments of code that are syntactically the same (as opposed to textually) are called *Type 2 clones*. Type 2 clones differ only in whitespace, comments, names of identifiers, and literals. Every Type 1 clone is always also a Type 2 clone, but some Type 2 clones are not Type 1 clones. The methods SetPageWidthInInches and SetPageWidthInPoints are Type 2 clones but not Type 1 clones.

The guideline presented in this chapter is about Type 1 clones, for two reasons:

- Source code maintenance benefits most from the removal of Type 1 clones.
- Type 1 clones are easier to detect and recognize (both by humans and computers, as detecting Type 2 clones requires full parsing).

The limit of six lines of code may appear somewhat arbitrary, since other books and tools use a different limit. In our experience, the limit of six lines is the right balance between identifying too many and too few clones. As an example, a `ToString` method could be three or four lines, and those lines may occur in many domain objects. Those clones can be ignored, as they are not what we are looking for—namely, deliberate copies of functionality.

4.1 Motivation

To understand the advantages of a codebase with little duplication, in this section we discuss the effects that duplication has on system maintainability.

Duplicated Code Is Harder to Analyze

If you have a problem, you want to know how to fix it. And part of that "how" is where to locate the problem. When you are calling an existing method, you can easily find the source. When you are copying code, the source of the problem may exist elsewhere as well. However, the only way to find out is by using a clone detection tool. A well-known tool for clone detection is CPD, which is included in a source code analysis tool called PMD (*https://pmd.github.io*). Several editions of Visual Studio come with a clone detection tool built-in.

 The fundamental problem of duplication is not knowing whether there is another copy of the code that you are analyzing, how many copies exist, and where they are located.

Duplicated Code Is Harder to Modify

All code may contain bugs. But if duplicated code contains a bug, the same bug appears multiple times. Therefore, duplicated code is harder to modify; you may need to repeat bug fixes multiple times. This, in turn, requires knowing that a fix has to be made in a duplicate in the first place! This is why duplication is a typical source of so-called *regression bugs*: functionality that has worked normally before suddenly stops working (because a duplicate was overlooked).

The same problem holds for regular changes. When code is duplicated, changes may need to be made in multiple places, and having many duplicates makes changing a codebase unpredictable.

4.2 How to Apply the Guideline

To avoid the problem of duplicated bugs, never reuse code by copying and pasting existing code fragments. Instead, put it in a method if it is not already in one, so that you can call it the second time that you need it. That is why, as we have covered in the previous chapters, the Extract Method refactoring technique is the workhorse that solves many duplication problems.

In the example presented at the beginning of the chapter, the code that implements the checksum (which is part of the duplicate) is an obvious candidate for extraction. To resolve duplication using Extract Method, the duplicate (or a part thereof) is extracted into a new method which is then called multiple times, once from each duplicate.

In Chapter 2, the new extracted method became a private method of the class in which the long method occurs. That does not work if duplication occurs across classes, as in CheckingAccount and SavingsAccount. One option in that case is to make the extracted method a method of a utility class. In the example, we already have an appropriate class for that (Accounts). So the new static method, IsValid, is simply a method of that class:

```
public static bool IsValid(string number)
{
    int sum = 0;
    for (int i = 0; i < number.Length; i++)
    {
        sum = sum + (9 - i) * (int)Char.GetNumericValue(number[i]);
    }
    return sum % 11 == 0;
}
```

This method is called in CheckingAccount:

```
public class CheckingAccount
{
    private int transferLimit = 100;

    public Transfer MakeTransfer(string counterAccount, Money amount)
    {
        // 1. Check withdrawal limit:
        if (amount.GreaterThan(this.transferLimit))
        {
            throw new BusinessException("Limit exceeded!");
        }
        if (Accounts.IsValid(counterAccount))
```

```
    { ❶
        // 2. Look up counter account and make transfer object:
        CheckingAccount acct = Accounts.FindAcctByNumber(counterAccount);
        Transfer result = new Transfer(this, acct, amount); ❷
        return result;
    }
    else
    {
        throw new BusinessException("Invalid account number!");
    }
        }
    }
}
```

❶ Start of short clone (three lines of code).

❷ End of short clone (three lines of code).

And also in **SavingsAccount**:

```
public class SavingsAccount
{
    public CheckingAccount RegisteredCounterAccount { get; set; }

    public Transfer MakeTransfer(string counterAccount, Money amount)
    {
        // 1. Assuming result is 9-digit bank account number, validate 11-test:
        if (Accounts.IsValid(counterAccount))
        { ❶
            // 2. Look up counter account and make transfer object:
            CheckingAccount acct = Accounts.FindAcctByNumber(counterAccount);
            Transfer result = new Transfer(this, acct, amount); ❷
            if (result.CounterAccount.Equals(this.RegisteredCounterAccount))
            {
                return result;
            }
            else
            {
                throw new BusinessException("Counter-account not registered!");
            }
        }
        else
        {
            throw new BusinessException("Invalid account number!!");
        }
    }
}
```

❶ Start of short clone (three lines of code).

❷ End of short clone (three lines of code).

Mission accomplished: according to the definition of duplication presented at the beginning of this chapter, the clone has disappeared (because the repeated fragment is fewer than six lines of code). But the following issues remain:

- Even though according to the definition, the clone has disappeared, there is still logic repeated in the two classes.

- The extracted fragment had to be put in a third class, just because in C# every method needs to be in a class (or struct). The class to which the extracted method was added runs the risk of becoming a hodgepodge of unrelated methods. This leads to a *large class smell* and *tight coupling*. Having a large class is a smell because it signals that there are multiple unrelated functionalities within the class. This tends to lead to tight coupling when methods need to know implementation details in order to interact with such a large class. (For elaboration, see Chapter 6.)

The refactoring technique presented in the next section solves these problems.

The Extract Superclass Refactoring Technique

In the preceding code snippets, there are separate classes for a checking account and a savings account. They are functionally related. However, they are not related in C# (they are just two classes that each derive directly from System.Object). Both have common functionality (the checksum validation), which introduced a duplicate when we created SavingsAccount by copying and pasting (and modifying) CheckingAccount. One could say that a checking account is a special type of a (general) bank account, and that a savings account is also a special type of a (general) bank account. C# (and other object-oriented languages) has a feature to represent the relationship between something general and something specific: inheritance from a superclass to a subclass.

The *Extract Superclass* refactoring technique uses this feature by extracting a fragment of code lines not just to a method, but to a new class that is the superclass of the original class. So, to apply this technique, you create a new Account class like so:

```csharp
public class Account
{
    public virtual Transfer MakeTransfer(string counterAccount, Money amount)
    {
        // 1. Assuming result is 9-digit bank account number, validate 11-test: ❶
        int sum = 0;
        for (int i = 0; i < counterAccount.Length; i++)
        {
            sum = sum + (9 - i) * (int)Char.
                GetNumericValue(counterAccount[i]);
        }
        if (sum % 11 == 0)
```

```
    {
        // 2. Look up counter account and make transfer object:
        CheckingAccount acct = Accounts.FindAcctByNumber(counterAccount);
        Transfer result = new Transfer(this, acct, amount); ❷
        return result;
    }
    else
    {
        throw new BusinessException("Invalid account number!");
    }
    }
}
```

❶ Start of extracted clone.

❷ End of extracted clone.

The new superclass, Account, contains logic shared by the two types of special accounts. You can now turn both the CheckingAccount and SavingsAccount classes into subclasses of this new superclass. For CheckingAccount, the result looks like this:

```
public class CheckingAccount : Account
{
    private int transferLimit = 100;

    public override Transfer MakeTransfer(string counterAccount, Money amount)
    {
        if (amount.GreaterThan(this.transferLimit))
        {
            throw new BusinessException("Limit exceeded!");
        }
        return base.MakeTransfer(counterAccount, amount);
    }
}
```

The CheckingAccount class declares its own member, transferLimit, and overrides MakeTransfer. The MakeTransfer method first checks to be sure the amount to be transferred does not exceed the limit for checking accounts. If that is the case, it calls MakeTransfer in the superclass to create the actual transfer.

The new version of SavingsAccount works likewise:

```
public class SavingsAccount : Account
{
    public CheckingAccount RegisteredCounterAccount { get; set; }

    public override Transfer MakeTransfer(string counterAccount, Money amount)
    {
        Transfer result = base.MakeTransfer(counterAccount, amount);
        if (result.CounterAccount.Equals(this.RegisteredCounterAccount))
        {
```

```
            return result;
        }
        else
        {
            throw new BusinessException("Counter-account not registered!");
        }
    }
}
```

The SavingsAccount class declares RegisteredCounterAccount and, just like Check
ingAccount, overrides MakeTransfer. The MakeTransfer method does not need to
check a limit (because savings accounts do not have a limit). Instead, it calls Make
Transfer directly in the superclass to create a transfer. It then checks whether the
transfer is actually with the registered counter account.

All functionality is now exactly where it belongs. The part of making a transfer that is
the same for all accounts is in the Account class, while the parts that are specific to
certain types of accounts are in their respective classes. All duplication has been
removed.

As the comments indicate, the MakeTransfer method in the Account superclass has
two responsibilities. Although the duplication introduced by copying and pasting
CheckingAccount has already been resolved, one more refactoring—extracting the
11-test to its own method—makes the new Account class even more maintainable:

```
public class Account
{
    public Transfer MakeTransfer(string counterAccount, Money amount)
    {
        if (IsValid(counterAccount))
        {
            CheckingAccount acct = Accounts.FindAcctByNumber(counterAccount);
            return new Transfer(this, acct, amount);
        }
        else
        {
            throw new BusinessException("Invalid account number!");
        }
    }

    public static bool IsValid(string number)
    {
        int sum = 0;
        for (int i = 0; i < number.Length; i++)
        {
            sum = sum + (9 - i) * (int)Char.GetNumericValue(number[i]);
        }
        return sum % 11 == 0;
    }
}
```

The `Account` class is now a natural place for `IsValid`, the extracted method.

4.3 Common Objections to Avoiding Code Duplication

This section discusses common objections regarding code duplication. From our experience, these are developers' arguments for allowing duplication, such as copying from other codebases, claiming there are "unavoidable" cases, and insisting that some code will "never change."

Copying from Another Codebase Should Be Allowed

"Copying and pasting code from another codebase is not a problem because it will not create a duplicate in the codebase of the current system."

Technically, that is correct: it does not create a duplicate in the codebase of the current system. Copying code from another system may seem beneficial if the code solves the exact same problem in the exact same context. However, in any of the following situations you will run into problems:

The other (original) codebase is still maintained
Your copy will not benefit from the improvements made in the original codebase. Therefore, do not copy, but rather import the functionality needed (that is, add the other codebase to your classpath).

The other codebase is no longer maintained and you are working on rebuilding this codebase
In this case, you definitely should not copy the code. Often, rebuilds are caused by maintainability problems or technology renewals. In the case of maintainability issues, you would be defeating the purpose by copying code. You are introducing code that is determined to be (on average) hard to maintain. In the case of technology renewals, you would be introducing limitations of the old technology into the new codebase, such as an inability to use abstractions that are needed for reusing functionality efficiently.

Slight Variations, and Hence Duplication, Are Unavoidable

"Duplication is unavoidable in our case because we need slight variations of common functionality."

Indeed, systems often contain slight variations of common functionality. For instance, some functionality is slightly different for different operating systems, for other versions (for reasons of backward compatibility), or for different customer groups. However, this does not imply that duplication is unavoidable. You need to find those parts of the code that are shared by all variants and move them to a common superclass, as in the examples presented in this chapter. You should strive to model variations in the code in such a way that they are explicit, isolated, and testable.

This Code Will Never Change

"This code will never, ever change, so there is no harm in duplicating it."

If it is absolutely, completely certain that code will never, ever change, duplication (and every other aspect of maintainability) is not an issue. For a start, you have to be absolutely, completely certain that the code in question also does not contain any bugs that need fixing. Apart from that, the reality is that systems change for many reasons, each of which may eventually lead to changes in parts deemed to never, ever change:

- The *functional requirements* of the system may change because of changing users, changing behavior, or a change in the way the organization does business.

- The *organization* may change in terms of ownership, responsibilities, development approach, development process, or legislative requirements.

- *Technology* may change, typically in the system's environment, such as the operating system, libraries, frameworks, or interfaces to other applications.

- *Code* itself may change, because of bugs, refactoring efforts, or even cosmetic improvements.

That is why we argue that most of the time the expectation that code never changes is unfounded. So accepting duplication is really nothing more than accepting the risk that someone else will have to deal with it later if it happens.

   Your code *will* change. Really.

Duplicates of Entire Files Should Be Allowed as Backups

"We are keeping copies of entire files in our codebase as backups. Every backup is an unavoidable duplicate of all other versions."

We recommend keeping backups, but not in the way implied by this objection (inside the codebase). Version control systems such as Microsoft TFS, SVN and Git provide a much better backup mechanism. If those are not available, move backup files to a directory next to the root of the codebase, not inside it. Why? Because sooner or later you will lose track of which variant of a file is the right one.

Unit Tests Are Covering Me

"Unit tests will sort out whether something goes wrong with a duplicate."

This is true only if the duplicates are in the same method, and the unit test of the method covers both. If the duplicates are in other methods, it can be true only if a code analyzer alerts you if duplicates are changing. Otherwise, unit tests would not necessarily signal that something is wrong if only one duplicate has changed. Hence, you cannot rely only on the tests (identifying symptoms) instead of addressing the root cause of the problem (using duplicate code). You should not assume that eventual problems will be fixed later in the development process, when you could avoid them altogether right now.

Duplication in String Literals Is Unavoidable and Harmless

"I need long string literals with a lot of duplication in them. Duplication is unavoidable and does not hurt because it is just in literals."

This is a variant of one of the objections discussed in Chapter 2 ("This unit is impossible to split"). We often see code that contains long SQL queries or XML or HTML documents appearing as string literals in C# code. Sometimes such literals are complete clones, but more often parts of them are repeated. For instance, we have seen SQL queries of more than a hundred lines of code that differed only in the sorting order (order by asc versus order by desc). This type of duplication is not harmless even though technically they are not in the C# logic itself. It is also not unavoidable; in fact this type of duplication can be avoided in a straightforward fashion:

- Extract to a method that uses string concatenation and parameters to deal with variants.
- Use a templating engine to generate HTML output from smaller, nonduplicated fragments that are kept in separate files.

4.4 See Also

Less duplication leads to a smaller codebase; for elaboration, see Chapter 9. See the Extract Method refactoring technique in Chapter 2 for splitting units to make them easier to reuse.

How SIG Rates Duplication

The amount of duplication is one of the eight system properties of the SIG/TÜViT Evaluation Criteria for Trusted Product Maintainability. To rate duplication, all Type 1 (i.e., textually equal) code clones of at least six lines of code are considered, except clones consisting entirely of `import` statements. Code clones are then categorized in two risk categories: redundant clones and nonredundant clones, as follows. Take a fragment of 10 lines of code that appears three times in the codebase. In other words, there is a group of three code clones, each 10 lines of code. Theoretically, two of these can be removed: they are considered technically redundant. Consequently, 10 + 10 = 20 lines of code are categorized as redundant. One clone is categorized as nonredundant, and hence, 10 lines of code are categorized as nonredundant. To be rated at 4 stars, at most 4.6% of the total number of lines of code in the codebase can be categorized as redundant. See Table 4-1

Table 4-1. Minimum thresholds for a 4-star duplication rating (2015 version of the SIG/ TÜViT Evaluation Criteria)

Lines of code categorized as …	Percentage allowed for 4 stars
… nonredundant	At least 95.4%
… redundant	At most 4.6%

See the three quality profiles in Figure 4-1 as an example:

- Left: an open source system, in this case Jenkins
- Center: an anonymous system in the SIG benchmark that complies with a 4-star rating for duplication
- Right: the cutoff points for achieving 4-star quality for this quality characteristic

Figure 4-1. Three code duplication quality profiles

CHAPTER 5

Keep Unit Interfaces Small

Bunches of data that hang around together really ought to be made into their own object.

—Martin Fowler

Guideline:

- **Limit the number of parameters per unit to at most 4.**
- Do this by **extracting parameters into objects**.
- This improves maintainability because keeping the number of parameters low **makes units easier to understand and reuse**.

There are many situations in the daily life of a programmer where long parameter lists seem unavoidable. In the rush of getting things done, you might add a few parameters more to that one method in order to make it work for exceptional cases. In the long term, however, such a way of working will lead to methods that are hard to maintain and hard to reuse. To keep your code maintainable it is essential to avoid long parameter lists, or *unit interfaces*, by limiting the number of parameters they have.

A typical example of a unit with many parameters is the render method in the Board Panel class of JPacman. This method renders a square and its occupants (e.g., a ghost, a pellet) in a rectangle given by the x,y,w,h parameters.

```
/// <summary>
/// Renders a single square on the given graphics context on the specified
/// rectangle.
///
/// <param name="square">The square to render.</param>
```

```
/// <param name="g">The graphics context to draw on.</param>
/// <param name="x">The x position to start drawing.</param>
/// <param name="y">The y position to start drawing.</param>
/// <param name="w">The width of this square (in pixels.)</param>
/// <param name="h">The height of this square (in pixels.)</param>
private void Render(Square square, Graphics g, int x, int y, int w, int h)
{
    square.Sprite.Draw(g, x, y, w, h);
    foreach (Unit unit in square.Occupants)
    {
        unit.Sprite.Draw(g, x, y, w, h);
    }
}
```

This method exceeds the parameter limit of 4. Especially the last four arguments, all of type int, make the method harder to understand and its usage more error-prone than necessary. It is not unthinkable that after a long day of writing code, even an experienced developer could mix up the x,y,w and h parameters—a mistake that the compiler and possibly even the unit tests will not catch.

Because the x,y,w, and h variables are related (they define a rectangle with a 2D anchor point, a width and a height), and the render method does not manipulate these variables independently, it makes sense to group them into an object of type Rectangle. The next code snippets show the Rectangle class and the refactored render method:

```
public class Rectangle
{
    public Point Position { get; set; }

    public int Width { get; set; }

    public int Height { get; set; }

    public Rectangle(Point position, int width, int height)
    {
        this.Position = position;
        this.Width = width;
        this.Height = height;
    }

}

/// <summary>
/// Renders a single square on the given graphics context on the specified
/// rectangle.
///
/// <param name="square">The square to render.</param>
/// <param name="g">The graphics context to draw on.</param>
/// <param name="r">The position and dimension for rendering the square.</param>
private void Render(Square square, Graphics g, Rectangle r)
```

```
{
    Point position = r.Position;
    square.Sprite.Draw(g, position.X, position.Y, r.Width, r.Height);
    foreach (Unit unit in square.Occupants)
    {
        unit.Sprite.Draw(g, position.X, position.Y, r.Width, r.Height);
    }
}
```

Now the render method has only three parameters instead of six. Next to that, in the whole system we now have the Rectangle class available to work with. This allows us to also create a smaller interface for the draw method:

```
private void Render(Square square, Graphics g, Rectangle r)
{
    Point position = r.Position;
    square.Sprite.Draw(g, r);
    foreach (Unit unit in square.Occupants)
    {
        unit.Sprite.Draw(g, r);
    }
}
```

The preceding refactorings are an example of the *Introduce Parameter Object* refactoring pattern. Avoiding long parameter lists, as shown in the previous example, improves the readability of your code. In the next section, we explain why small interfaces contribute to the overall maintainability of a system.

5.1 Motivation

As we already discussed in the introduction, there are good reasons to keep interfaces small and to introduce suitable objects for the parameters you keep passing around in conjunction. Methods with small interfaces keep their context simple and thus are easier to understand. Furthermore, they are easier to reuse and modify because they do not depend on too much external input.

Small Interfaces Are Easier to Understand and Reuse

As the codebase grows, the core classes become the API upon which a lot of other code in the system builds. In order to keep the volume of the total codebase low (see also Chapter 9) and the speed of development high, it is important that the methods in the core classes have a clear and small interface. Suppose you want to store a Pro ductOrder object in the database: would you prefer a ProductOrderDao.store(Pro ductOrder order) method or a ProductOrderDao.store(ProductOrder order, String databaseUser, String databaseName, boolean validateBeforeStore, boolean closeDbConnection) method?

Methods with Small Interfaces Are Easier to Modify

Large interfaces do not only make your methods obscure, but in many cases also indicate multiple responsibilities (especially when you feel that you really cannot group your objects together anymore). In this sense, interface size correlates with unit size and unit complexity. So it is pretty obvious that methods with large interfaces are hard to modify. If you have, say, a method with eight parameters and a lot is going on in the method body, it can be difficult to see where you can split your method into distinct parts. However, once you have done so, you will have several methods with their own responsibility, and moreover, each method will have a small number of parameters! Now it will be much easier to modify each of these methods, because you can more easily locate exactly where your modification needs to be done.

5.2 How to Apply the Guideline

By the time you have read this, you should be convinced that having small interfaces is a good idea. How small should an interface be? In practice, an upper bound of four seems reasonable: a method with four parameters is still reasonably clear, but a method with five parameters is already getting difficult to read and has too many responsibilities.

So how can you ensure small interfaces? Before we show you how you can *fix* methods with large interfaces, keep in mind that large interfaces are not the problem, but rather are *indicators* of the actual problem—a poor data model or ad hoc code modification. So, you can view interface size as a code smell, to see whether your data model needs improvement.

Large interfaces are usually not the main problem; rather, they are a code smell that indicates a deeper maintainability problem.

Let us say you have a `buildAndSendMail` method that takes a list of nine parameters in order to construct and send an email message. However, if you looked at just the parameter list, it would not be very clear what would happen in the method body:

```
public void DoBuildAndSendMail(MailMan m, string firstName, string lastName,
    string division, string subject, MailFont font, string message1,
    string message2, string message3)
{
    // Format the email address
    string mId = $"{firstName[0]}.{lastName.Substring(0, 7)}" +
        $"@{division.Substring(0, 5)}.compa.ny";
    // Format the message given the content type and raw message
    MailMessage mMessage = FormatMessage(font,
```

```
        message1 + message2 + message3);
    // Send message
    m.Send(mId, subject, mMessage);
    }
```

The `buildAndSendMail` method clearly has too many responsibilities; the construction of the email address does not have much to do with sending the actual email. Furthermore, you would not want to confuse your fellow programmer with five parameters that together will make up a message body! We propose the following revision of the method:

```
public void DoBuildAndSendMail(MailMan m, MailAddress mAddress,
    MailBody mBody)
{
    // Build the mail
    Mail mail = new Mail(mAddress, mBody);
    // Send the mail
    m.SendMail(mail);
}

public class Mail
{
    public MailAddress Address { get; set; }
    public MailBody Body { get; set; }

    public Mail(MailAddress mAddress, MailBody mBody)
    {
        this.Address = mAddress;
        this.Body = mBody;
    }
}

public class MailBody
{
    public string Subject { get; set; }
    public MailMessage Message { get; set; }

    public MailBody(string subject, MailMessage message)
    {
        this.Subject = subject;
        this.Message = message;
    }
}

public class MailAddress
{
    public string MsgId { get; private set; }

    public MailAddress(string firstName, string lastName,
        string division)
    {
        this.MsgId = $"{firstName[0]}.{lastName.Substring(0, 7)}" +
```

```
                    $"@{division.Substring(0, 5)}.compa.ny";
        }
    }
```

The `buildAndSendMail` method is now considerably less complex. Of course, you now have to construct the email address and message body before you invoke the method. But if you want to send the same message to several addresses, you only have to build the message once, and similarly for the case where you want to send a bunch of messages to one email address. In conclusion, we have now separated concerns, and while we did so we introduced some nice, structured classes.

The examples presented in this chapter all group parameters into objects. Such objects are often called *data transfer objects* or *parameter objects*. In the examples, these new objects actually represent meaningful concepts from the domain. A point, a width, and a height represent a rectangle, so grouping these in a class called `Rectangle` makes sense. Likewise, a first name, a last name, and a division make an address, so grouping these in a class called `MailAddress` makes sense, too. It is not unlikely that these classes will see a lot of use in the codebase because they are useful generalizations, not just because they may decrease the number of parameters of a method.

What if we have a number of parameters that do not fit well together? We can always make a parameter object out of them, but probably, it will be used only once. In such cases, another approach is often possible, as illustrated by the following example.

Suppose we are creating a library that can draw charts, such as bar charts and pie charts, on a `System.Drawing.Graphics` canvas. To draw a nice-looking chart, you usually need quite a bit of information, such as the size of the area to draw on, configuration of the category axis and value axis, the actual dataset to chart, and so forth. One way to supply this information to the charting library is like this:

```
public static void DrawBarChart(Graphics g,
    CategoryItemRendererState state,
    Rectangle graphArea,
    CategoryPlot plot,
    CategoryAxis domainAxis,
    ValueAxis rangeAxis,
    CategoryDataset dataset)
{
    // ..
}
```

This method already has seven parameters, three more than the guideline presented in this chapter allows. Moreover, any call to `drawBarChart` needs to supply values for all seven parameters. What if the charting library provided default values wherever possible? One way to implement this is to use method overloading and define, for instance, a two-parameter version of `drawBarChart`:

```
public static void DrawBarChart(Graphics g, CategoryDataset dataset)
{
    Charts.DrawBarChart(g,
        CategoryItemRendererState.DEFAULT,
        new Rectangle(new Point(0, 0), 100, 100),
        CategoryPlot.DEFAULT,
        CategoryAxis.DEFAULT,
        ValueAxis.DEFAULT,
        dataset);
}
```

This covers the case where we want to use defaults for all parameters whose data types have a default value defined. However, that is just one case. Before you know it, you are defining more than a handful of alternatives like these. And the version with seven parameters is still there.

Another way to solve this is to use the *Replace Method with Method Object* refactoring technique presented in Chapter 2. This refactoring technique is primarily used to make methods shorter, but it can also be used to reduce the number of method parameters.

To apply the Replace Method with Method Object technique to this example, we define a BarChart class like this:

```
public class BarChart
{
    private CategoryItemRendererState state =
        CategoryItemRendererState.DEFAULT;
    private Rectangle graphArea = new Rectangle(new Point(0, 0), 100, 100);
    private CategoryPlot plot = CategoryPlot.DEFAULT;
    private CategoryAxis domainAxis = CategoryAxis.DEFAULT;
    private ValueAxis rangeAxis = ValueAxis.DEFAULT;
    private CategoryDataset dataset = CategoryDataset.DEFAULT;

    public BarChart Draw(Graphics g)
    {
        // ..
        return this;
    }

    public ValueAxis GetRangeAxis()
    {
        return rangeAxis;
    }

    public BarChart SetRangeAxis(ValueAxis rangeAxis)
    {
        this.rangeAxis = rangeAxis;
        return this;
    }

    // More getters and setters.
```

```
    }
```

The static method `drawBarChart` from the original version is replaced by the (non-static) method `draw` in this class. Six of the seven parameters of `drawBarChart` have been turned into of `BarChart` class. All of these have default values. We have chosen to keep parameter g (of type `System.Drawing.Graphics`) as a parameter of `draw`. This is a sensible choice: `draw` always needs a `Graphics` object, and there is no sensible default value. But it is not necessary: we could also have made g into the seventh private member and supplied a getter and setter for it.

We made another choice: all setters return `this` to create what is called a *fluent interface*. The setters can then be called in a cascading style, like so:

```
private void ShowMyBarChart()
{
    Graphics g = this.CreateGraphics();
    BarChart b = new BarChart()
        .SetRangeAxis(myValueAxis)
        .SetDataset(myDataset)
        .Draw(g);
}
```

In this particular call of `draw`, we provide values for the range axis, dataset, and g, and use default values for the other members of `BarChart`. We could have used more default values or fewer, without having to define additional overloaded `draw` methods.

5.3 Common Objections to Keeping Unit Interfaces Small

It may take some time to get rid of all large interfaces. Typical objections to this effort are discussed next.

Objection: Parameter Objects with Large Interfaces

"The parameter object I introduced now has a constructor with too many parameters."

If all went well, you have grouped a number of parameters into an object during the refactoring of a method with a large interface. It may be the case that your object now has a lot of parameters because they apparently fit together. This usually means that there is a finer distinction possible inside the object. Remember the first example, where we refactored the `render` method? Well, the defining parameters of the rectangle were grouped together, but instead of having a constructor with four arguments we actually put the x and y parameters together in the `Point` object. So, in general, you should not refuse to introduce a parameter object, but rather think about the structure of the object you are introducing and how it relates to the rest of your code.

Refactoring Large Interfaces Does Not Improve My Situation

"When I refactor my method, I am still passing a lot of parameters to another method."

Getting rid of large interfaces is not always easy. It usually takes more than refactoring one method. Normally, you should continue splitting responsibilities in your methods, so that you access the most primitive parameters only when you need to manipulate them separately. For instance, the refactored version of the render method needs to access all parameters in the Rectangle object because they are input to the draw method. But it would be better, of course, to also refactor the draw method to access the x,y,w, and h parameters inside the method body. In this way, you have just passed a Rectangle in the render method, because you do not actually manipulate its class variables before you begin drawing!

Frameworks or Libraries Prescribe Interfaces with Long Parameter Lists

"The interface of a framework we're using has nine parameters. How can I implement this interface without creating a unit interface violation?"

Sometimes frameworks/libraries define interfaces or classes with methods that have long parameter lists. Implementing or overriding these methods will inevitably lead to long parameter lists in your own code. These types of violations are impossible to prevent, but their impact can be limited. To limit the impact of violations caused by third-party frameworks or libraries, it is best to isolate these violations—for instance, by using wrappers or adapters. Selecting a different framework/library is also a viable alternative, although this can have a large impact on other parts of the codebase.

5.4 See Also

Methods with multiple responsibilities are more likely when the methods are large and complex. Therefore, make sure that you understand the guidelines for achieving short and simple units. See Chapters 2 and 3.

How SIG Rates Unit Interfacing

Unit interfacing is one of the eight system properties of the SIG/TÜViT Evaluation Criteria for Trusted Product Maintainability. To rate unit interfacing, every unit of the system is categorized in one of four risk categories depending on its number of parameters. Table 5-1 lists the four risk categories used in the 2015 version of the SIG/TÜViT Evaluation Criteria.

Table 5-1. Minimum thresholds for a 4-star unit size rating (2015 version of the SIG/TÜViT Evaluation Criteria)

Lines of code in methods with …	Percentage allowed for 4 stars for unit interfacing
… more than seven parameters	At most 0.7%
… five or more parameters	At most 2.7%
… three or more parameters	At most 13.8%
… at most two parameters	At least 86.2%

See the three quality profiles shown in Figure 5-1 as an example:

- Left: an open source system, in this case Jenkins
- Center: an anonymous system in the SIG benchmark that complies with a 4-star rating for unit interfacing
- Right: the cutoff points for achieving 4-star quality for this quality characteristic

Figure 5-1. Three quality profiles for unit interfacing

CHAPTER 6

Separate Concerns in Modules

In a system that is both complex and tightly coupled, accidents are inevitable.

—Charles Perrow's Normal Accidents theory in one sentence

Guideline:

- **Avoid large modules in order to achieve loose coupling between them**.
- Do this by **assigning responsibilities to separate modules and hiding implementation details behind interfaces**.
- This improves maintainability because changes in a loosely coupled codebase are much **easier to oversee and execute** than changes in a tightly coupled codebase.

The guidelines presented in the previous chapters are all what we call *unit guidelines*: they address improving maintainability of individual units (methods/constructors) in a system. In this chapter, we move up from the unit level to the module level.

Remember that the concept of a module translates to a class in object-oriented languages such as C#.

This module-level guideline addresses relationships between classes. This guideline is about achieving loose coupling.

We will use a true story to illustrate what tight coupling between classes is and why it leads to maintenance problems. This story is about how a class called UserService in the service layer of a web application started growing while under development and kept on growing until it violated the guideline of this chapter.

In the first development iteration, the UserService class started out as a class with only three methods, the names and responsibilities of which are shown in this code snippet:

```
public class UserService
{
    public User LoadUser(string userId)
    {
        // ...
    }

    public bool DoesUserExist(string userId)
    {
        // ...
    }

    public User ChangeUserInfo(UserInfo userInfo)
    {
        // ...
    }
}
// end::UserSerice[]
}
```

In this case, the backend of the web application provides a REST interface to the frontend code and other systems.

A REST interface is an approach for providing web services in a simplified manner. REST is a common way to expose functionality outside of the system. The class in the REST layer that implements user operations uses the UserService class like this:

```
public class UserController : System.Web.Http.ApiController
{

    private readonly UserService userService = new UserService();

    // ...

    public System.Web.Http.IHttpActionResult GetUserById(string id)
    {
        User user = userService.LoadUser(id);
        if (user == null)
        {
            return NotFound();
        }
        return Ok(user);
```

```
        }
    }
```

During the second development iteration, the UserService class is not modified at all. In the third development iteration, new requirements were implemented that allowed a user to register to receive certain notifications. Three new methods were added to the UserService class for this requirement:

```csharp
public class UserService
{
    public User LoadUser(string userId)
    {
        // ...
    }

    public bool DoesUserExist(string userId)
    {
        // ...
    }

    public User ChangeUserInfo(UserInfo userInfo)
    {
        // ...
    }

    public List<NotificationType> GetNotificationTypes(User user)
    {
        // ...
    }

    public void RegisterForNotifications(User user, NotificationType type)
    {
        // ...
    }

    public void UnregisterForNotifications(User user, NotificationType type)
    {
        // ...
    }
}
// end::UserSerice[]
```

```
}
```

These new functionalities were also exposed via a separate REST API class:

```csharp
public class NotificationController : System.Web.Http.ApiController
{
    private readonly UserService userService = new UserService();

    // ...

    public System.Web.Http.IHttpActionResult Register(string id,
```

```
        string notificationType)
{
    User user = userService.LoadUser(id);
    userService.RegisterForNotifications(user,
        NotificationType.FromString(notificationType));
    return Ok();
}

[System.Web.Http.HttpPost]
[System.Web.Http.ActionName("unregister")]
public System.Web.Http.IHttpActionResult Unregister(string id,
    string notificationType)
{
    User user = userService.LoadUser(id);
    userService.UnregisterForNotifications(user,
        NotificationType.FromString(notificationType));
    return Ok();
}
}
```

In the fourth development iteration, new requirements for searching users, blocking users, and listing all blocked users were implemented (management requested that last requirement for reporting purposes). All of these requirements caused new methods to be added to the UserService class.

```
public class UserService
{
    public User LoadUser(string userId)
    {
        // ...
    }

    public bool DoesUserExist(string userId)
    {
        // ...
    }

    public User ChangeUserInfo(UserInfo userInfo)
    {
        // ...
    }

    public List<NotificationType> GetNotificationTypes(User user)
    {
        // ...
    }

    public void RegisterForNotifications(User user, NotificationType type)
    {
        // ...
    }
```

```
        public void UnregisterForNotifications(User user, NotificationType type)
        {
            // ...
        }

        public List<User> SearchUsers(UserInfo userInfo)
        {
            // ...
        }

        public void BlockUser(User user)
        {
            // ...
        }

        public List<User> GetAllBlockedUsers()
        {
            // ...
        }
    }
    // end::UserSerice[]

}
```

At the end of this development iteration, the class had grown to an impressive size. At this point the UserService class had become the most used service in the service layer of the system. Three frontend views (pages for Profile, Notifications, and Search), connected through three REST API services, used the UserService class. The number of incoming calls from other classes (the *fan-in*) has increased to over 50. The size of class has increased to more than 300 lines of code.

These kind of classes have what is called the *large class smell*, briefly discussed in Chapter 4. The code contains too much functionality and also knows implementation details about the code that surrounds it. The consequence is that the class is now *tightly coupled*. It is called from a large number of places in the code, and the class itself *knows* details on other parts of the codebase. For example, it uses different data layer classes for user profile management, the notification system, and searching/blocking other users.

Coupling means that two parts of a system are somehow connected when changes are needed. That may be direct calls, but classes could also be connected via a configuration file, database structure, or even assumptions they make (in terms of business logic).

The problem with these classes is that they become a maintenance hotspot. All functionalities related (even remotely) to users are likely to end up in the UserService class. This is an example of an improper *separation of concerns*. Developers will also find the UserService class increasingly more difficult to understand as it becomes large and unmanageable. Less experienced developers on the team will find the class intimidating and will hesitate to make changes to it.

Two principles are necessary to understand the significance of coupling between classes.

- Coupling is an issue on the class level of source code. Each of the methods in UserService complies with all guidelines presented in the preceding chapters. However, it is the *combination* of methods in the UserService class that makes UserService tightly coupled with the classes that use it.

- Tight and loose coupling are a matter of degree. The actual maintenance consequence of tight coupling is determined by the *number of calls* to that class and the *size* of that class. Therefore, the more calls to a particular class that is tightly coupled, the smaller its size should be. Consider that even when classes are split up, the number of calls may not necessarily be lower. However, the coupling is then lower, because less code is coupled.

6.1 Motivation

The biggest advantage of keeping classes small is that it provides a direct path toward loose coupling between classes. Loose coupling means that your class-level design will be much more flexible to facilitate future changes. By "flexibility" we mean that you can make changes while limiting unexpected effects of those changes. Thus, loose coupling allows developers to work on isolated parts of the codebase without creating change ripples that affect the rest of the codebase. A third advantage, which cannot be underestimated, is that the codebase as a whole will be much more open to less experienced developers.

The following sections discuss the advantages of having small, loosely coupled classes in your system.

Small, Loosely Coupled Modules Allow Developers to Work on Isolated Parts of the Codebase

When a class is tightly coupled with other classes, changes to the implementation of the class tend to create ripple effects through the codebase. For example, changing the interface of a public method leads to code changes everywhere the method is called. Besides the increased development effort, this also increases the risk that class modifications lead to bugs or inconsistencies in remote parts of the codebase.

Small, Loosely Coupled Modules Ease Navigation Through the Codebase

Not only does a good separation of concerns keep the codebase flexible to facilitate future changes, it also improves the analyzability of the codebase since classes encapsulate data and implement logic to perform a single task. Just as it is easier to name methods that only do one thing, classes also become easier to name and understand when they have one responsibility. Making sure classes have only one responsibility is also known as the *single responsibility principle*.

Small, Loosely Coupled Modules Prevent No-Go Areas for New Developers

Classes that violate the *single responsibility principle* become tightly coupled and accumulate a lot of code over time. As with the UserService example in the introduction of this chapter, these classes become intimidating to less experienced developers, and even experienced developers are hesitant to make changes to their implementation. A codebase that has a large number of classes that lack a good separation of concerns is very difficult to adapt to new requirements.

6.2 How to Apply the Guideline

In general, this guideline prescribes keeping your classes small (by addressing only one concern) and limiting the number of places where a class is called by code outside the class itself. Following are three development best practices that help to prevent tight coupling between classes in a codebase.

Split Classes to Separate Concerns

Designing classes that collectively implement functionality of a software system is the most essential step in modeling and designing object-oriented systems. In typical software projects we see that classes start out as logical entities that implement a single functionality but over time gain more responsibilities. To prevent classes from getting a *large class smell*, it is crucial that developers take action if a class has more than one responsibility by splitting up the class.

To demonstrate how this works with the UserService class from the introduction, we split the class into three separate classes. Here are the two newly created classes and the modified UserService class:

```
public class UserNotificationService
{
    public IList<NotificationType> GetNotificationTypes(User user)
    {
        // ...
```

```
        }

        public void Register(User user, NotificationType type)
        {
            // ...
        }

        public void Unregister(User user, NotificationType type)
        {
            // ...
        }
    }
    public class UserBlockService
    {
        public void BlockUser(User user)
        {
            // ...
        }

        public IList<User> GetAllBlockedUsers()
        {
            // ...
        }
    }
    public class UserService
    {
        public User LoadUser(string userId)
        {
            // ...
        }

        public bool DoesUserExist(string userId)
        {
            // ...
        }

        public User ChangeUserInfo(UserInfo userInfo)
        {
            // ...
        }

        public IList<User> SearchUsers(UserInfo userInfo)
        {
            // ...
        }
    }
```

After we rewired the calls from the REST API classes, the system now has a more loosely coupled implementation. For example, the UserService class has no knowledge about the notification system or the logic for blocking users. Developers are also more likely to put new functionalities in separate classes instead of defaulting to the `UserService` class.

Hide Specialized Implementations Behind Interfaces

We can also achieve loose coupling by *hiding* specific and detailed implementations behind a high-level interface. Consider the following class, which implements the functionality of a digital camera that can take snapshots with the flash on or off:

```
public class DigitalCamera
{
    public Image TakeSnapshot()
    {
        // ...
    }

    public void FlashLightOn()
    {
        // ...
    }

    public void FlashLightOff()
    {
        // ...
    }
}
```

And suppose this code runs inside an app on a smartphone device, like this:

```
public class SmartphoneApp
{
    private static DigitalCamera camera = new DigitalCamera();

    public static void Main(string[] args)
    {
        // ...
        Image image = camera.TakeSnapshot();
        // ...
    }
}
```

A more advanced digital camera becomes available. Apart from taking snapshots, it can also record video, has a timer feature, and can zoom in and out. The `DigitalCamera` class is extended to support the new features:

```
public class DigitalCamera
{
    public Image TakeSnapshot()
    {
        // ...
    }
```

```csharp
    public void FlashLightOn()
    {
        // ...
    }

    public void FlaslLightOff()
    {
        // ...
    }

    public Image TakePanoramaSnapshot()
    {
        // ...
    }

    public Video Record()
    {
        // ...
    }

    public void SetTimer(int seconds)
    {
        // ...
    }

    public void ZoomIn()
    {
        // ...
    }

    public void ZoomOut()
    {
        // ...
    }
}
```

From this example implementation, it is not difficult to imagine that the extended version of the DigitalCamera class will be much larger than the initial version, which has fewer features.

The codebase of the smartphone app still uses only the original three methods. However, because there is still just one DigitalCamera class, the app is forced to use this larger class. This introduces more coupling in the codebase than necessary. If one (or more) of the additional methods of DigitalCamera changes, we have to review the codebase of the smartphone app, only to find that it is not affected. While the smartphone app does not use any of the new methods, they are available to it.

To lower coupling, we use an interface that defines a limited list of camera features implemented by both basic and advanced cameras:

```
public interface ISimpleDigitalCamera
{
    Image TakeSnapshot();

    void FlashLightOn();

    void FlashLightOff();
}
public class DigitalCamera : ISimpleDigitalCamera
{
    // ...
}
public class SmartphoneApp
{
    private static ISimpleDigitalCamera camera = SDK.GetCamera();

    public static void Main(string[] args)
    {
        // ...
        Image image = camera.TakeSnapshot();
        // ...
    }
}
```

This change leads to lower coupling by a higher degree of encapsulation. In other words, classes that use only basic digital camera functionalities now do not know about all of the advanced digital camera functionalities. The SmartphoneApp class accesses only the SimpleDigitalCamera interface. This *guarantees* that Smart phoneApp does not use any of the methods of the more advanced camera.

Also, this way your system becomes more *modular*: it is composed such that a change to one class has minimal impact on other classes. This, in turn, increases *modifiability*: it is easier and less work to modify the system, and there is less risk that modifications introduce defects.

Replace Custom Code with Third-Party Libraries/Frameworks

A third situation that typically leads to tight module coupling are classes that provide generic or utility functionality. Classic examples are classes called StringUtils and FileUtils. Since these classes provide generic functionality, they are obviously called from many places in the codebase. In many cases this is an occurrence of tight coupling that is hard to avoid. A best practice, though, is to keep the class sizes limited and to periodically review (open source) libraries and frameworks to check if they can replace the custom implementation. CommonLibrary.NET (*https://commonlibrar ynet.codeplex.com/*) is a widespread library with frequently used utility functionality. In some cases, utility code can be replaced with new C# language features or a company-wide shared library.

6.3 Common Objections to Separating Concerns

The following are typical objections to the principle explained in this chapter.

Objection: Loose Coupling Conflicts With Reuse

"Tight coupling is a side effect of code reuse, so this guideline conflicts with that best practice."

Of course, code reuse can increase the number of calls to a method. However, there are two reasons why this should not lead to tight coupling:

- Reuse does not necessarily lead to methods that are called from as many places as possible. Good software design—for example, using inheritance and hiding implementation behind interfaces—will stimulate code reuse while keeping the implementation loosely coupled, since interfaces hide implementation details.

- Making your code more generic, to solve more problems with less code, does not mean it should become a tightly coupled codebase. Clearly, utility functionality is expected to be called from more places than specific functionality. Utility functionality should then also embody less source code. In that way, there may be many incoming dependencies, but the dependencies refer to a small amount of code.

Objection: C# Interfaces Are Not Just for Loose Coupling

"It doesn't make sense to use C# interfaces to prevent tight coupling."

Indeed, using interfaces is a great way to improve encapsulation by hiding implementations, but it does not make sense to provide an interface for every class. As a rule of thumb, an interface should be implemented by at least two classes in your codebase. Consider splitting your class if the only reason to put an interface in front of your class is to limit the amount of code that other classes see.

Objection: High Fan-in of Utility Classes Is Unavoidable

"Utility code will always be called from many locations in the codebase."

That is true. In practice, even highly maintainable codebases contain a small amount of code that is so generic that it is used by many places in the codebase (for example, logging functionality or I/O code). Highly generic, reusable code should be small, and some of it may be unavoidable. However, if the functionality is indeed that common, there may be a framework or library available that already implements it and can be used as is.

Objection: Not All Loose Coupling Solutions Increase Maintainability

"Frameworks that implement inversion of control (IoC) achieve loose coupling but make it harder to maintain the codebase."

Inversion of control is a design principle to achieve loose coupling. There are frameworks available that implement this for you. IoC makes a system more flexible for extension and decreases the amount of knowledge that pieces of code have of each other.

This objection holds when such frameworks add complexity for which the maintaining developers are not experienced enough. Therefore, in cases where this objection is true, it is not IoC that is the problem, but the framework that implements it.

Thus, the design decision to use a framework for implementing IoC should be considered with care. As with all engineering decisions, this is a trade-off that does not pay off in all cases. Using these types of frameworks just to achieve loose coupling is a choice that can almost never be justified.

How SIG Rates Module Coupling

Module coupling is one of the eight system properties of the SIG/TÜViT Evaluation Criteria for Trusted Product Maintainability. To rate module coupling, the fan-in of every method is calculated. Each module (class in C#) is then categorized in one of four risk categories depending on the total fan-in of all methods in the class. Table 6-1 lists the four risk categories used in the 2015 version of the SIG/TÜViT Evaluation Criteria. The table shows the maximum amount of code that may fall in the risk categories in order to achieve a 4-star rating. For example, a maximum of 21.8% of code volume may be in classes with a fan-in in the moderate risk category, and likewise for the other risk categories.

Table 6-1. Module coupling risk categories (2015 version of the SIG/TÜViT Evaluation Criteria)

Fan-in of modules in the category	Percentage allowed for 4 stars
51+	At most 6.6%
21–50	At most 13.8%
11–20	At most 21.6%
1–10	No constraint

See the three quality profiles in Figure 6-1 as an example:

- Left: an open source system, in this case Jenkins. Note that Jenkins does not fulfill the 4-star requirement here for the highest risk category (in red).

- Center: an anonymous system in the SIG benchmark that complies with a 4-star rating for module coupling.

- Right: the cutoff points for achieving 4-star quality for this quality characteristic.

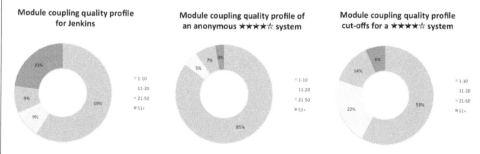

Figure 6-1. Three quality profiles for module coupling

CHAPTER 7

Couple Architecture Components Loosely

There are two ways of constructing a software design: one way is to make it so simple that there are obviously no deficiencies, and the other way is to make it so complicated that there are no obvious deficiencies.

—C.A.R. Hoare

Guideline:

- **Achieve loose coupling between top-level components**.
- Do this by **minimizing the relative amount of code within modules that is exposed to (i.e., can receive calls from) modules in other components**.
- This improves maintainability because **independent components ease isolated maintenance**.

Having a clear view on software architecture is essential when you are building and maintaining software. A good software architecture gives you insight into what the system does, how the system does it, and how functionality is organized (in component groupings, that is). It shows you the high-level structure, the "skeleton" so to speak, of the system. Having a good architecture makes it easier to find the source code that you are looking for and to understand how (high-level) components interact with other components.

This chapter deals with dependencies on the component level. A component is part of the top-level division of a system. It is defined by a system's software architecture, so its boundaries should be quite clear from the start of development. As it is touching upon the software architecture domain, it may be outside of your direct control.

However, the implementation of software architecture always remains the responsibility of you as a developer.

Components should be *loosely coupled*; that is, they should be clearly separated by having few entry points for other components and a limited amount of information shared among components. In that case, implementation details of methods are hidden (or encapsulated) which makes the system more modular.

Sounds familiar? Yes, both as a general design principle and on a module level, loose coupling has been discussed in Chapter 6. Component coupling applies the same reasoning but at the higher level of components rather than modules. Module coupling focuses on the exposure of individual modules (classes) to the rest of the codebase. Component coupling focuses specifically on the exposure of modules in one component (group of modules) to the modules in *another component*.

 So a module being called from a module in the same component is considered to be an internal call if we assess at the component level, but when we assess it at the module level, there is *module coupling* indeed.

In this chapter, we refer to the characteristic of being loosely coupled on a component level as *component independence*. The opposite of component *in*dependence is component *dependence*. In that case, the inner workings of components are exposed too much to other components that rely on them. That kind of entanglement makes it harder to oversee effects that code changes in one component may have on others, because it does not behave in an isolated manner. This complicates testing, when we must make assumptions or simulations of what happens within another component.

7.1 Motivation

System maintenance is easier when changes within a component have effects that are isolated within that component. To clarify the advantages of having loosely coupled components, let us elaborate on the consequences of different types of dependencies with Figure 7-1.

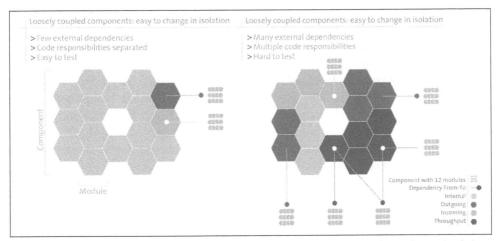

Figure 7-1. Low component dependence (left) and high component dependence (right)

The left side of the figure shows a low level of component dependence. Most calls between modules are internal (within the component). Let us elaborate on internal and noninternal dependencies.

Calls that improve maintainability:

- *Internal calls* are healthy. Since the modules calling each other are part of the same component, they should implement closely related functionality. Their inner logic is hidden from the outside.

- *Outgoing calls* are also healthy. As they delegate tasks to other components, they create a dependency outward. In general, delegation of distinct concerns to other components is a good thing. Delegation can be done from anywhere within a component and does not need to be restricted to a limited set of modules within the component.

 Note that outgoing calls from one component are incoming calls for another component.

Calls that have a negative impact on maintainability:

- *Incoming calls* provide functionality for other components by offering an interface. The code volume that is involved in this should be limited. Conversely, the code within a component should be encapsulated as much as possible—that is, it should be shielded against direct invocations from other components. This improves information hiding. Also, modifying code involved in incoming dependencies potentially has a large impact on other components. By having a small percentage of code involved in incoming dependencies, you may dampen the negative ripple effects of modifications to other components.

- *Throughput code* is risky and must be avoided. Throughput code both receives incoming calls and delegates to other components. Throughput code accomplishes the opposite of information hiding: it exposes its delegates (implementation) to its clients. It is like asking a question to a help desk that does not formulate its own answer but instead forwards your question to another company. Now you are dependent on two parties for the answer. In the case of code, this indicates that responsibilities are not well divided over components. As it is hard to trace back the path that the request follows, it is also hard to test and modify: tight coupling may cause effects to spill over to other components.

The right side of the figure shows a component with a high level of component dependence. The component has many dependencies with modules outside the component and is thus tightly coupled. It will be hard to make isolated changes, since the effects of changes cannot be easily overseen.

 Note that the effects of component independence are enhanced by *component balance*. Component balance is achieved when the number of components and their relative size are balanced. For elaboration on this topic, see Chapter 8.

To give you an idea of how coupling between components evolves over time, consider how entanglements seem to appear naturally in systems. Entanglements evolve over time because of hasty hacks in code, declining development discipline, or other reasons why the intended architecture cannot be applied consistently. Figure 7-2 illustrates a situation that we encounter often in our practice. A system has a clear architecture with one-way dependencies, but over time they become blurred and entangled. In this case, the entanglement is between layers, but similar situations occur between components.

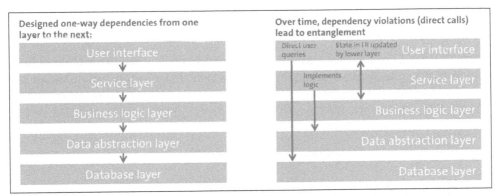

Figure 7-2. Designed versus implemented architecture

Low Component Dependence Allows for Isolated Maintenance

A low level of dependence means that changes can be made in an isolated manner. This applies when most of a component's code volume is either *internal* or *outgoing*. Isolated maintenance means less work, as coding changes do not have effects outside the functionality that you are modifying.

> Note that this reasoning about isolation applies to code on a smaller level. For example, a system consisting of small, simple classes signals a proper separation of concerns, but does not guarantee it. For that, you will need to investigate the actual dependencies (see, for example, Chapter 6).

Low Component Dependence Separates Maintenance Responsibilities

If all components are independent from each other, it is easier to distribute responsibilities for maintenance among separate teams. This follows from the advantage of isolated modification. Isolation is in fact a prerequisite for efficient division of development work among team members or among different teams.

By contrast, if components are tightly intertwined with each other, one cannot isolate and separate maintenance responsibilities among teams, since the effects of modifications will spill over to other teams. Aside from that code being hard to test, the effects of modifications may also be unpredictable. So, dependencies may lead to inconsistencies, more time spent on communication between developers, and time wasted waiting for others to complete their modifications.

Low Component Dependence Eases Testing

Code that has a low dependence on other components (modules with mainly *internal* and *outgoing* code) is easier to test. For internal calls, functionality can be traced and tested within the component. For outgoing calls, you do not need to mock or stub functionality that is provided by other components (given that functionality in that other component is finished).

For elaboration on (unit) testing, see also Chapter 10.

7.2 How to Apply the Guideline

The goal for this chapter's guideline is to achieve loose coupling between components. In practice, we find that you can help yourself by adhering to the following principles for implementing interfaces and requests between components.

The following principles help you apply the guideline of this chapter:

- Limit the size of modules that are the component's interface.
- Define component interfaces on a high level of abstraction. This limits the types of requests that cross component borders. That avoids requests that "know too much" about the implementation details.
- Avoid throughput code, because it has the most serious effect on testing functionality. In other words, avoid interface modules that put through calls to other components. If throughput code exists, analyze the concerned modules in order to solve calls that are put through to other components.

Abstract Factory Design Pattern

Component independence reflects the high-level architecture of a software system. However, this is not a book on software architecture. In this section, we discuss only one design pattern that we frequently see applied in practice to successfully limit the amount of interface code exposed by a component: the *Abstract Factory design pattern*. A system that is loosely coupled is characterized by relying more on contracts and less on implementation details.

Many more design patterns and software architecture styles can help in keeping your architecture components loosely coupled. An example is using a framework for *dependency injection* (which allows *Inversion of Control*). For elaboration on other patterns, we kindly direct you to the many great books on design patterns and software architecture (see, for example, "Related Books" on page xiv).

The Abstract Factory design pattern hides (or *encapsulates*) the creation of specific "products" behind a generic "product factory" interface. In this context, products are typically entities for which more than one variant exists. Examples are audio format decoder/encoder algorithms or user interface widgets that have different themes for "look and feel." In the following example, we use the Abstract Factory design patten to encapsulate the specifics of cloud hosting platforms behind a small factory interface.

Suppose our codebase contains a component, called PlatformServices, that implements the management of services from a cloud hosting platform. Two specific cloud hosting providers are supported by the PlatformServices component: Amazon AWS and Microsoft Azure (more could be added in the future).

To start/stop servers and reserve storage space, we have to implement the following interface for a cloud hosting platform:

```
public interface ICloudServerFactory
{
    ICloudServer LaunchComputeServer();

    ICloudServer LaunchDatabaseServer();

    ICloudStorage CreateCloudStorage(long sizeGb);
}
```

Based on this interface, we create two specific factory classes for AWS and Azure:

```
public class AWSCloudServerFactory : ICloudServerFactory
{
    public ICloudServer LaunchComputeServer()
    {
        return new AWSComputeServer();
    }

    public ICloudServer LaunchDatabaseServer()
    {
        return new AWSDatabaseServer();
    }

    public ICloudStorage CreateCloudStorage(long sizeGb)
    {
        return new AWSCloudStorage(sizeGb);
    }
}
public class AzureCloudServerFactory : ICloudServerFactory {
    public ICloudServer LaunchComputeServer() {
        return new AzureComputeServer();
    }

    public ICloudServer LaunchDatabaseServer() {
```

```
        return new AzureDatabaseServer();
    }

    public ICloudStorage CreateCloudStorage(long sizeGb) {
        return new AzureCloudStorage(sizeGb);
    }
}
```

Note that these factories make calls to specific AWS and Azure implementation classes (which in turn do specific AWS and Azure API calls), but return generic interface types for servers and storage.

Code outside the `PlatformServices` component can now use the concise interface module `ICloudServerFactory`—for example, like this:

```
public class ApplicationLauncher
{

    public static void Main(string[] args)
    {
        ICloudServerFactory factory;
        if (args[1].Equals("-azure"))
        {
            factory = new AzureCloudServerFactory();
        }
        else
        {
            factory = new AWSCloudServerFactory();
        }
        ICloudServer computeServer = factory.LaunchComputeServer();
        ICloudServer databaseServer = factory.LaunchDatabaseServer();
```

The `ICloudServerFactory` interface of the `PlatformServices` provides a small interface for other components in the codebase. This way, these other components can be loosely coupled to it.

7.3 Common Objections to Loose Component Coupling

This section discusses objections regarding component dependence, whether they concern the difficulty of fixing the component dependence itself, or dependency being a requirement within the system.

Objection: Component Dependence Cannot Be Fixed Because the Components Are Entangled

"We cannot get component dependence right because of mutual dependencies between components."

Entangled components are a problem that you experience most clearly during maintenance. You should start by analyzing the modules in the *throughput* category, as it has the most serious effect on the ease of testing and on predicting what exactly the functionality does.

When you achieve clearer boundaries for component responsibilities, it improves the analyzability and testability of the modules within. For example, modules with an extraordinary number of incoming calls may signal that they have multiple responsibilities and can be split up. When they are split up, the code becomes easier to analyze and test. For elaboration, please refer to Chapter 6.

Objection: No Time to Fix

"In the maintenance team, we understand the importance of achieving low component dependence, but we are not granted time to fix it."

We understand how this is an issue. Development deadlines are real, and there may not be time for refactoring, or what a manager may see as "technical aesthetics." What is important is the trade-off. One should resolve issues that pose a real problem for maintainability. So dependencies should be resolved if the team finds that they inhibit testing, analysis, or stability. You can solidify your case by measuring what percentage of issues arises/maintenance effort is needed in components that are tightly coupled with each other.

For example, throughput code follows complex paths that are hard to test for developers. There may be more elegant solutions that require less time and effort.

Objection: Throughput Is a Requirement

"We have a requirement for a software architecture for a layer that puts through calls."

It is true that some architectures are designed to include an intermediate layer. Typically, this is a service layer that collects requests from one side (e.g., the user interface) and bundles them for passing on to another layer in the system. The existence of such a layer is not necessarily a problem—given that this layer implements loose coupling. It should have a clear separation of incoming and outgoing requests. So the module that receives requests in this layer:

- Should not process the request itself.
- Should not know where and how to process that request (its implementation details).

If both are true, the receiving module in the service layer has an incoming request and an outgoing request, instead of putting requests through to a specific module in the receiving component.

A large-volume service layer containing much logic is a typical code smell. In that case, the layer does not merely abstract and pass on requests, but also transforms them. Hence, for transformation, the layer knows about the implementation details. That means that the layer does not properly encapsulate both request and implementation. If throughput code follows from software architecture requirements, you may raise the issue to the software or enterprise architect.

7.4 See Also

A related concept to component independence is that of component balance, discussed in Chapter 8. That chapter deals with achieving an overseeable number of components that are balanced in size.

How SIG Rates Component Independence

SIG defines and measures loose coupling between components as "component independence." The independence is measured on the module level, as each module in a system should be contained in a component. "Module" here is the smallest grouping of code units, typically a file.

You can assess dependence between modules by measuring calls between them (in static source code analysis). For classifying dependence between components, we make a distinction between *hidden* code and *interface* code.

- *Hidden code* is composed of modules that have no incoming dependencies from modules in other components: they call only within their own component (*internal*) and may have calls outside their own component (*outgoing* calls).
- *Interface* code is composed of modules that have incoming dependencies from modules in other components. They consist of code in modules with *incoming* and *throughput* code.

Following the principle of loose coupling, a low level of dependence between modules is better than a high level of dependence. That signals the risk that changes within one component propagate to other components.

SIG measures component independence as the percentage of code that is classified as *hidden code*. To achieve a SIG/TÜViT rating of 4 stars for highly-maintainable software, the percentage of code residing in modules with incoming dependencies from other components (*incoming* or *throughput*) should not exceed 14.2%.

See the three quality profiles in Figure 7-3 as an example:

- Left: an open source system, in this case Jenkins
- Center: an anonymous system in the SIG benchmark that complies with a 4-star rating for component independence
- Right: the cutoff points for achieving 4-star quality for this quality characteristic

Figure 7-3. Three quality profiles for component independence

CHAPTER 8

Keep Architecture Components Balanced

Building encapsulation boundaries is a crucial skill in software architecture.

—George H. Fairbanks in *Just Enough Architecture*

Guideline:

- **Balance the number and relative size of top-level components** in your code.

- Do this by **organizing source code in a way that the number of components is close to 9** (i.e., between 6 and 12) and that the **components are of approximately equal size**.

- This improves maintainability because balanced components **ease locating code and allow for isolated maintenance**.

A well-balanced software architecture is one with not too many and not too few components, with sizes that are approximately equal. The architecture then has a good *component balance*.

An example of *component imbalance* would be having a few very large components that contain a disproportionate amount of system logic and many small ones that dwindle in comparison.

Figure 8-1 gives an impression of component balance and what the ideal situation would be. The least desirable situation is on the top left because changes cannot be made in an isolated component. The ideal situation is shown last, the one with nine components in which it is most likely that maintenance can be isolated to one or two components that have a limited scope. The second situation (top right) suffers from a skewed distribution of volume over components. When one component is extraordinarily large, the architecture becomes monolithic; it becomes hard to navigate the codebase and do isolated maintenance. In the third situation (bottom left), where the architecture is scattered among many components, it becomes hard to keep a mental map of the codebase and to grasp how components interact.

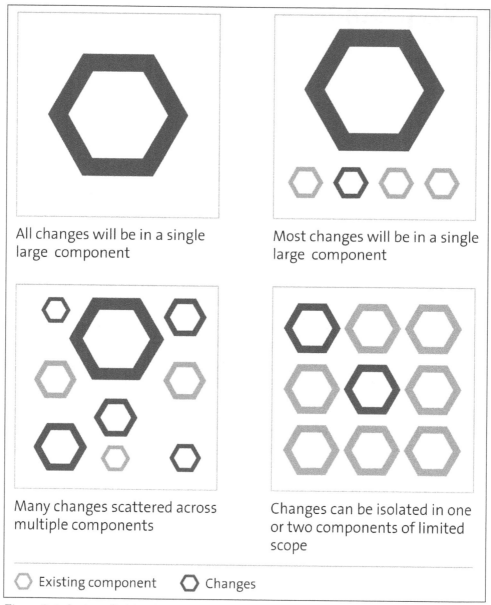

Figure 8-1. *System division in components, with worst component balance top-left and best component balance bottom-right*

8.1 Motivation

Now we know what component balance *is*, but not why it is important. The reason is simple: software maintenance is easier when the software architecture is balanced. This section discusses in what ways you can benefit from a good system component balance: it makes it easier to find and analyze code, it better isolates effects of maintenance, and it separates maintenance responsibilities.

A Good Component Balance Eases Finding and Analyzing Code

A clear code organization in components makes it easier to find the piece of code that you want to change. Of course, proper code hygiene helps in this process as well, such as using a consistent naming convention (see Chapter 11). When the number of components is manageable (around nine) and their volume is consistent, they allow for a drill-down each time that you need to analyze code to modify it.

In contrast, an unbalanced organization of components is more likely to have unclear functional boundaries. For example, a component that is very large compared to others is more likely to contain functionalities that are unrelated, and therefore that component is harder to analyze.

A Good Component Balance Better Isolates Maintenance Effects

When a system's component balance clearly describes functional boundaries, it has a proper *separation of concerns*, which makes for isolated behavior in the system. Isolated behavior within system components is relevant because it guards against unexpected effects, such as regression.

More broadly, isolation of code within components has the general advantage of modularity: components with clear functional and technical boundaries are easier to substitute, remove, and test than components with mixed functionalities and technical intertwinement.

Note that a good component balance in itself clearly does not guarantee isolation of changes. After all, grouping code in different components does not necessarily make those components independent from each other. So, the degree of dependence between components is relevant as well, as we will discuss in Chapter 7.

This reasoning about isolation applies to code on a smaller level as well. For example, a system that consists of small, simple classes signals a proper separation of concerns, but does not guarantee it. For that you will need to investigate the actual dependencies (see, e.g., Chapter 6).

A Good Component Balance Separates Maintenance Responsibilities

Having clear functional boundaries between components makes it easier to distribute responsibilities for maintenance among separate teams. The number of components of a system and their relative size should indicate the system's decomposition into functional groups.

When a system has too many or too few components, it is considered more difficult to understand and harder to maintain. If the number of components is too low, it does not help you much to navigate through the functionalities of the system. On the other hand, too many components make it hard to get a clear overview of the entire system.

8.2 How to Apply the Guideline

The two principles of component balance are:

- The number of top-level system components should ideally be 9, and generally between 6 and 12.

- The components' volume in terms of source code should be roughly equal.

Note that component balance is an *indicator* for a clear component separation, not a goal in itself. It should follow from the system design and development process. The division of the system into components should be natural, not forced to nine components for the sake of having nine components.

Decide on the Right Conceptual Level for Grouping Functionality into Components

To achieve a good system division that is easy to navigate for developers, you need to choose the right conceptual level for grouping functionality. Usually, software systems are organized along high-level functional domains that describe what kind of functions the system performs for the user. Alternatively, a division is made along the separations of technical specialities.

For example, a system that bases component division on function domains might have components like Data Retrieval, Invoice Administration, Reporting, Administrator, and so on. Each component contains source code that offers end-to-end functionality, ranging from the database to the frontend. A functional division has the advantage of being available during design, before development starts. For developers, it has the advantage that they can analyze source code while thinking in high-level functionalities. A disadvantage can be that developers may need to be proficient and comfortable in multiple technical domains to make changes to a single component.

An example of a system that uses technical division might have components like Frontend, Backend, Interfaces, Logging, and so on. This approach has advantages for teams that have a division of responsibilities based on technology specialization. The component division then reflects the division of labor among various specialists.

Choosing the right concepts for grouping functionality within a system is part of the software architect role. This role may be assigned to a single person, or it may be distributed over various people within the development team. When changes are needed to the component division, those in the architect role must be consulted.

Clarify the System's Domains and Apply Those Consistently

Once a choice for the type of system division into components has been made, you need to apply it consistently. An inconsistent architecture is a bad architecture. Therefore, the division into components should be formalized and controlled. While making the design choices may be an architect's role, the discipline to create and respect the component boundaries in the code organization applies to all developers. A way to achieve this is to agree as a team in which components certain changes need to be implemented. It is a collective responsibility to ensure that this is done in a consistent manner.

8.3 Common Objections to Balancing Components

This section discusses objections regarding component balance. Common objections are that component imbalance is not really a problem, or that it is a problem that cannot be fixed.

Objection: Component Imbalance Works Just Fine

"Our system may seem to have bad component balance, but we're not having any problems with it."

Component balance, as we define it, is not binary. There are different degrees of balance, and its definition allows for some deviation from the "ideal" of nine components of equal size. Whether a component imbalance is an actual maintenance burden depends on the degree of deviation, the experience of the maintenance team, and the cause of the imbalance.

The most important maintenance burden occurs when the imbalance is caused by lack of discipline during maintenance—when developers do not put code in the component where it belongs. Since inconsistency is the enemy of predictability, that may lead to unexpected effects. Code that is placed in the wrong components may lead to unintended dependencies between components, which hurts testability and flexibility.

Objection: Entanglement Is Impairing Component Balance

"We cannot get component balance right because of entanglement among components."

This situation points to another problem: technical dependence between components. Entanglement between components signals an improper separation of concerns. This issue and guideline are further described in Chapter 7. In this case, it is more important and urgent to fix component dependencies—for example, by hiding implementation details behind interfaces and fixing circular dependencies. After that, you can revise your component structure to improve its balance.

8.4 See Also

Component coupling is closely related to the idea of component balance discussed in this chapter. Component coupling is discussed in Chapter 7.

How SIG Rates Component Balance

SIG defines and measures component balance as a combined calculation (i.e., multiplication) of the following:

- The number of top-level system components
- The uniformity of component size

The ideal *number of top-level system components* is nine, as SIG has identified that as the median in its benchmark. The closer the actual number of components is to nine, the better.

The score for the number of top-level system components ranges from 0 to 1. A system with nine components gives a score of 1, linearly decreasing to 0 for a system with one component. A correction is applied upward, to allow for a more lenient count when the number of components is higher than 17, which would otherwise lead to a score of 0 with a linear model. The correction is based on the 95th percentile scores within the benchmark.

Uniformity of component size means the distribution of source code volume between components. An equally sized distribution of top-level components is better than an unequal distribution.

SIG uses the adjusted Gini coefficient as a measure of component size uniformity. The Gini coefficient measures the inequality of distribution between things and ranges from 0 (perfect equality) to 1 (perfect inequality).

To achieve a SIG/TÜViT rating of 4 stars for highly-maintainable software, the number of components should be close to the ideal of nine, and the adjusted Gini coefficient of the component sizes should be 0.71 maximum.

See the volume charts in Figure 8-2 as an example:

- Left: an anonymous system in the SIG benchmark that scores 2 stars on component balance. Note that both the number of components (six) and their code volume are off.
- Right: an anonymous system in the SIG benchmark that complies with a 4-star rating for component balance. Note that even though the volume of the components is not equal, the number of components is exactly nine, which levels out the influence of the component size inequality.

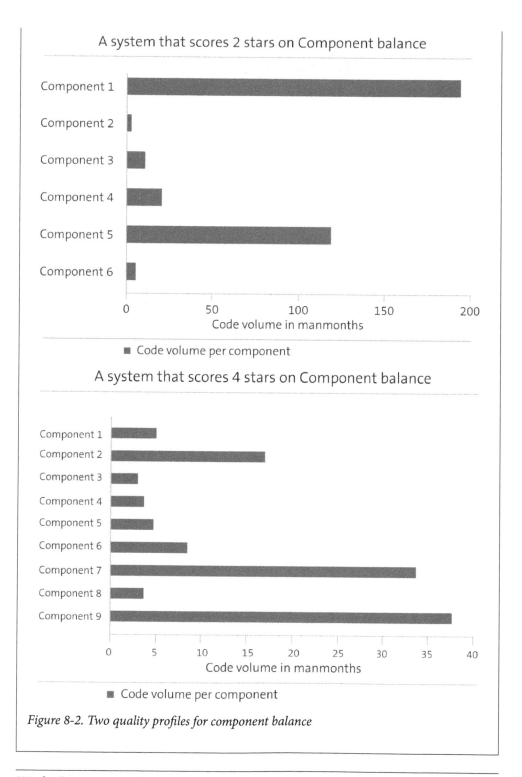

Figure 8-2. Two quality profiles for component balance

CHAPTER 9

Keep Your Codebase Small

Program complexity grows until it exceeds the capability of the programmer who must maintain it.

—7th Law of Computer Programming

Guideline:

- **Keep your codebase as small as feasible**.
- Do this by **avoiding codebase growth and actively reducing system size**.
- This improves maintainability because having a **small product, project, and team is a success factor**.

A *codebase* is a collection of source code that is stored in one repository, can be compiled and deployed independently, and is maintained by one team. A system has at least one codebase. Larger systems sometimes have more than one codebase. A typical example is packaged software. There may be a codebase for the standard functionality, and there are different, independently maintained codebases for customer- or market-specific plugins.

Given two systems with the same functionality, in which one has a small codebase and the other has a large codebase, you surely would prefer the small system. In a small system it is easier to search through, analyze, and understand code. If you modify something, it is easier to tell whether the change has effects elsewhere in the system. This ease of maintenance leads to fewer mistakes and lower costs. That much is obvious.

9.1 Motivation

Software development and maintenance become increasingly hard with growing system size. Building larger systems requires larger teams and longer-lasting projects, which bring additional overhead and risks of (project) failure. The rest of this section discusses the adverse effects of large software systems.

A Project That Sets Out to Build a Large Codebase Is More Likely to Fail

There is a strong correlation between project size and project risks. A large project leads to a larger team, complex design, and longer project duration. As a result, there is more complex communication and coordination among stakeholders and team members, less overview over the software design, and a larger number of requirements that change during the project. This all increases the chance of reduced quality, project delays, and project failure. The probabilities in the graph in Figure 9-1 are cumulative: for example, for all projects over 500 man-years of development effort, more than 90% are indentified as "poor project quality." A subset of this is projects with delays (80–90% of the total) and failed projects (50% of the total).

Figure 9-1 illustrates the relationship between project size and project failure: it shows that as the size of a project increases, the chances of project failure (i.e., project is terminated or does not deliver results), of project delay, and of a project delivered with poor quality are increasingly high.

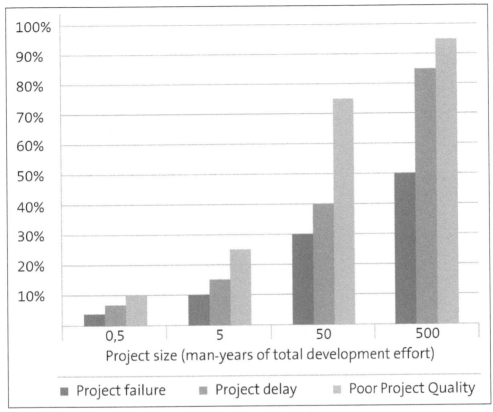

Figure 9-1. Probability of project failures by project size[1]

---

1 Source: *The Economics of Software Quality* by Capers Jones and Olivier Bonsignour (Addison-Wesley Professional 2012). The original data is simplified into man-years (200 function points/year for Java).

Large Codebases Are Harder to Maintain

Figure 9-2 illustrates how codebase size affects maintainability.

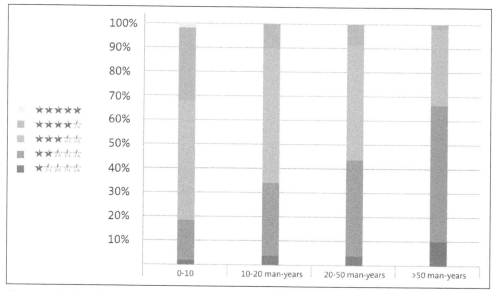

Figure 9-2. Distribution of system maintainability in SIG benchmark among different volume groups

The graph is based on a set of codebases of over 1,500 systems in the SIG Software Analysis Warehouse. Volume is measured as the amount of development effort in man-years to reproduce the system (see also "How SIG Rates Codebase Volume" on page 110). Each bar shows the distribution of systems in different levels of maintainability (benchmarked in stars). As the graph shows, over 30% of systems in the smallest volume category manage to reach 4- or 5-star maintainability, while in the largest volume category only a tiny percentage reaches this level.

Large Systems Have Higher Defect Density

You may expect that a larger system has more defects in absolute numbers. But the defect *density* (defined as the number of defects per 1,000 lines of code) also increases substantially as systems grow larger. Figure 9-3 shows the relationship between code volume and the number of defects per 1,000 lines of code. Since the number of defects rises when code volume grows, the graph shows that larger systems have higher defects both absolutely and relatively.

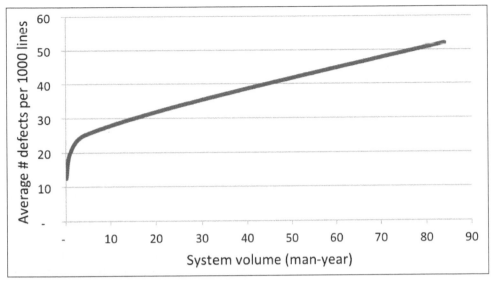

Figure 9-3. Impact of code volume on the number of defects[2]

9.2 How to Apply the Guideline

All other things being equal, a system that has less *functionality* will be smaller than a system that has more functionality. Then, the *implementation* of that functionality may be either concise or verbose. Therefore, achieving a small codebase first requires keeping the functionality of a system limited, and then requires attention to keep the amount of code limited.

Functional Measures

Functionality-related measures are not always within your span of control, but whenever new or adapted functionality is being discussed with developers, the following should be considered:

Fight scope creep:
> In projects, scope creep is a common phenomenon in which requirements extend during development. This may lead to "nice-to-have functionality" that adds growth to the system without adding much value to the business or the user. Fight scope creep by confronting the business with the price of additional functionality, in terms of project delays or higher future maintenance costs.

---

2 Source: Steve McConnell, *Code Complete*, 2nd edition (Microsoft Press, 2004), p.652.

Standardize functionality:

By *standardization of functionality* we mean consistency in the behavior and interactions of the program. First of all, this is intended to avoid the implementation of the same core functionality in multiple, slightly different ways. Secondly, standardization of functionality offers possibilities for reuse of code—assuming the code itself is written in a reusable way.

Technical Measures

For the technical implementation, the goal is to use less code to implement the same functionality. You can achieve this mainly through reusing code by referral (instead of writing or copying and pasting code again) or by avoiding coding altogether, but using existing libraries or frameworks.

Do not copy and paste code:

Referring to existing code is always preferable to copying and pasting code in pieces that will need to be maintained individually. If there are multiple copies of a piece of code, maintenance needs to occur in multiple places, too. Mistakes easily crop up if an update in one piece of logic requires individual adjustment (or not) and testing of multiple, scattered copies. Note that the intention of the guideline presented in Chapter 4 is precisely to avoid copying and pasting.

Refactor existing code:

While refactoring has many merits for code maintainability, it can have an immediate and visible effect in reducing the codebase. Typically, refactoring involves revisiting code, simplifying its structure, removing code redundancies, and improving the amount of reuse. This may be as simple as removing unused/obsolete functionality. See, for example, the refactoring patterns in Chapter 4.

Use third-party libraries and frameworks:

Many applications share the same type of behavior for which a vast number of frameworks and libraries exist—for example, UI behavior (e.g., jQuery (*http://jquery.com/*)), database access (e.g., Hibernate (*http://hibernate.org/*)), security measurements (e.g., Spring Security (*http://projects.spring.io/spring-security/*)), logging (e.g., SLF4J (*http://www.slf4j.org/*)), or utilities (e.g., Google Guava (*https://github.com/google/guava*)). Using third-party libraries is especially helpful for such generic functionality. If functionality is used and maintained by other parties, why invent your own? Using third-party code is especially helpful because it avoids unnecessary over-engineering. It is well worth considering adjusting functionality to fit it to third-party code instead of building a custom solution.

Do not make changes to the source code of a third-party library. If you do, essentially you have made the library code part of your own codebase. In particular, updates of changed libraries are cumbersome and can easily lead to bugs. Typically, difficulties arise when developers try to update the library to a newer version, since they need to analyze what has been changed in the library code and how that impacts the locally changed code.

Split up a large system:

Splitting up a large system into multiple smaller systems is a way to minimize the issues that come with larger systems. A prerequisite is that the system can be divided into parts that are independent, from a functional, technical, and lifecycle perspective. To the users, the systems (or plugins) must be clearly separated. Technically, the code in the different systems must be loosely coupled; that is, their code is related via interfaces instead of direct dependencies. Systems are only really independent if their lifecycles are decoupled (i.e., they are developed and released independently). Note that the split systems may well have some mutual or shared dependencies. There is an additional advantage. It might turn out that some of the new subsystems can be replaced by a third-party package, completely removing the need to have any codebase for this subsystem. An example is a Linux distribution such as Ubuntu. The Linux kernel is a codebase that lives at kernel.org and is maintained by a large team of volunteers headed by Linus Torvalds. Next to the actual Linux kernel, a distribution contains thousands of other software applications, each of which has its own codebase. These are the types of plugins that we mean here.

Decoupling (on a code level) is discussed in more detail in the chapters that deal with loose coupling, particularly Chapter 7.

9.3 Common Objections to Keeping the Codebase Small

The measures described in this chapter are applicable to all phases of software development. They support the primary maintainability goal of achieving a small codebase.

There are generally two familiar strategies with which you can actively pursue the goal of a small codebase: *avoiding* the problem (avoiding further codebase growth) or *fixing* the problem (reducing the size of the codebase).

The biggest long-term gains are achieved when you are working on a system that is already quite small or in an early stage of development. Technical adjustments such as refactoring and reuse of functionality are easier with a small system and will be beneficial for all further coding.

The most visible improvements will appear once a system is big and parts of it can be removed—for example, when functionality is being replaced by third-party code or after a system has been split into multiple parts.

Objection: Reducing the Codebase Size Is Impeded by Productivity Measures

"I cannot possibly reduce the size of my system, since my programming productivity is being measured in terms of added code volume."

If this is the case, we suggest escalating this issue. Measuring development productivity in terms of added code volume is a bad practice. It provides a negative incentive, as it encourages the bad habit of copying and pasting code. Code reference is better because it improves analyzing, testing, and changing code.

We understand that the number of code additions can help managers monitor progress and predict timelines. However, productivity should be measured in terms of *value* added, not *lines of code* added. Experienced developers can often add functionality with a minimum number of additional lines of code, and they will refactor the code whenever they see an opportunity, often resulting in *reduction* of the code size.

Objection: Reducing the Codebase Size is Impeded by the Programming Language

"I work with a language that is more verbose than others, so I cannot achieve a small codebase."

In most projects, the programming language is a given. It may very well be true that in some programming languages, it is impossible to get a small codebase (SQL-based languages come to mind). However, you can always strive to get a smaller codebase than you currently have, in the same programming language. Every codebase benefits from decreasing its size, even those in low-level languages with little possibility for abstraction.

Objection: System Complexity Forces Code Copying

"My system is so complicated that we can only add functionality by copying large pieces of existing code. Hence, it is impossible to keep the codebase small."

Difficulty in understanding existing code, and hence the fear of touching that code, is a common reason that programmers resort to copying and pasting. This is particularly the case if the code has an insufficient number of automated tests.

The best approach here is to find the functionality that is most like the one that you are trying to add. By analyzing that code, you should find some common functionality; otherwise, you would not consider copying that code in the first place. If that original functionality can be split up into multiple parts, then ideally you end up with a piece of code that can be referred to independently by the new functionality, avoiding duplication and taming codebase growth. Write unit tests for the new units to verify that you understand the inner workings of the unit. Besides, it is recommended practice; see Chapter 10.

Objection: Splitting the Codebase Is Impossible Because of Platform Architecture

"We cannot split the system into smaller parts because we are building for a platform where all functionality is tied to a common codebase."

Yes, platform-based software tends to grow large over time because it assimilates new functionality and rarely reduces functionality. One way to dramatically decrease the size of the codebase is to decouple the system into a plug-in architecture. This leads to multiple codebases that are each smaller than the original one. There is a codebase for the common core, and one or more codebases for the plugins. If those plugins are technically decoupled, they allow for separate release cycles. That means that small changes in functionality do not need an update of the whole system. Keep in mind that those small updates still need full integration/regression tests to ensure that the system as a whole still functions as expected.

Objection: Splitting the Codebase Leads to Duplication

"Splitting the codebase forces me to duplicate code."

There may be cases in which decoupling a system into separate parts (such as plugins/extensions) requires (interfaces to) common functionality or data structures to be duplicated in those extensions.

In such a case, duplication is a bigger problem than having a large codebase, and the guideline of Chapter 4 prevails over this guideline of achieving a small codebase. It is then preferable to code common functionality either as a separate extension or as part of a common codebase.

Objection: Splitting the Codebase Is Impossible Because of Tight Coupling

"I cannot split up my system since the system parts are tightly coupled."

Then decouple the system first. To achieve this, you can write specific interfaces that act as a uniform entry point to functionality. This can be achieved with WebServices, REST APIs, or other tooling that provides that functionality (e.g., middleware or ESB).

Keep in mind that the goal is to have subsystems that can be *maintained* independently, not necessarily systems that *operate* independently.

How SIG Rates Codebase Volume

The metric for codebase volume does not have different risk categories, since it consists of only one metric. To be rated at 4 stars, the codebase should be at most equivalent to 20 man-years of rebuild value. If C# is the only technology in a system, this translates to at most 160,000 lines of code.

Man-months and man-years

The total volume in a codebase is the volume in lines of code converted to man-months. A man-month is a standard measure of source code volume. It is the amount of source code that one developer with average productivity could write in one month. The advantage of "man-month" is that it allows for comparisons of source code volume between technologies. This is relevant because programming languages have different productivity measures, or "levels of verbosity." Therefore, a system with multiple programming languages can be converted to an aggregate measure that tells you the approximate effort it would take to rebuild it: the "rebuild value."

SIG's experience has shown that the man-month is an effective metric to assess the size of a system and to compare systems with each other. A man-*year* is simply 12 man-months. Of course, actual productivity is also dependent on skill and programming style. The volume metric does not tell you how many months or years of effort actually went into building the system.

CHAPTER 10

Automate Tests

Keep the bar green to keep the code clean.

—The jUnit motto

Guideline:

- **Automate tests for your codebase**.
- Do this by **writing automated tests using a test framework**.
- This improves maintainability because automated testing **makes development predictable and less risky**.

In Chapter 4, we have presented `IsValid`, a method to check whether bank account numbers comply with a checksum. That method contains a small algorithm that implements the checksum. It is easy to make mistakes in a method like this. That is why probably every programmer in the world at some point has written a little, one-off program to test the behavior of such a method, like so:

```csharp
using System;
using eu.sig.training.ch04.v1;

namespace eu.sig.training.ch10
{
    public class Program
    {
        [STAThread]
        public static void Main(string[] args)
        {
            string acct;
            do
            {
```

```
        Console.WriteLine("Type a bank account number on the next line.");
        acct = Console.ReadLine();
        Console.WriteLine($"Bank account number '{acct}' is" +
            (Accounts.IsValid(acct) ? "" : " not") + " valid.");
      } while (!String.IsNullOrEmpty(acct));
    }
  }
}
```

This is a C# class with a `Main` method, so it can be run from the command line:

```
C:\> Program.exe
Type a bank account number on the next line.
123456789
Bank account number '123456789' is valid.
Type a bank account number on the next line.
123456788
Bank account number '123456788' is not valid.
C:\>
```

A program like this can be called a *manual unit test*. It is a unit test because it is used to test just one unit, `IsValid`. It is manual because the user of this program has to type in test cases manually, and manually assess whether the output of the program is correct.

While better than having no unit testing at all, this approach has several problems:

- Test cases have to be provided by hand, so the test cannot be executed automatically in an easy way.

- The developer who has written this test is focusing on logic to execute the test (the `do … while` loop, all input/output handling), not on the test itself.

- The program does not show how `IsValid` is expected to behave.

- The program is not recognizable as a test (although the rather generic name `Program` is an indication it is meant as a one-off experiment).

That is why you should write automated unit tests instead of manual unit tests. These are tests of code units themselves described in code that runs autonomously. The same holds for other types of testing, such as regression tests and user acceptance tests: automate as much as possible, using a standard *test framework*. For unit tests, a common framework is NUnit (*http://nunit.org*).

10.1 Motivation

This section describes the advantages of *automating* your tests as much as possible.

Automated Testing Makes Testing Repeatable

Just like other programs and scripts, automated tests are executed in exactly the same way every time they are run. This makes testing repeatable: if a certain test executes at two different points in time yet gives different answers, it cannot be that the test execution itself was faulty. One can conclude that something has changed in the system that has caused the different outcome. With manual tests, there is always the possibility that tests are not performed consistently or that human errors are made.

Automated Testing Makes Development Efficient

Automated tests can be executed with much less effort than manual tests. The effort they require is negligible and can be repeated as often as you see fit. They are also faster than manual code review. You should also test as early in the development process as possible, to limit the effort it takes to fix problems.

 Postponing testing to a late stage in the development pipeline risks late identification of problems. That costs more effort to fix, because code needs to go back through the development pipeline and be merged, and tests must be rerun.

Automated Testing Makes Code Predictable

Technical tests can be automated to a high degree. Take unit tests and integration tests: they test the technical inner workings of code and the cohesion/integration of that code. Without being sure of the inner workings of your system, you might get the right results by accident. It is a bit like driving a car: you might arrive at an intended destination by following the wrong directions, but when you want to go to another destination, you are uncertain whether the new directions are reliable and will actually take you there.

A common advantage of automated testing is identifying when regression is occurring. Without a batch of automated unit tests, development quickly turns into a game of whack-a-mole: you implement a change in one piece of code, and while you are working on the next change in another piece of code, you realize you have introduced a bug with your previous change. Automated tests allow you to double-check your entire codebase effortlessly before turning to the next change. And since the automated unit tests follow predefined paths, you can be sure that if you have fixed a bug, it does not pop up on a second run.

Thus, running automated tests provides certainty about how the code works. There-fore, the predictability of automated tests also makes the quality of developed code more predictable.

Tests Document the Code That Is Tested

The script or program code of a test contains assertions about the expected behavior of the system under test. For example, as will be illustrated later in this chapter, an appropriate test of `IsValid` contains the following line of code: `Assert.IsFalse(IsValid(""))`. This documents, in C# code, that we expect `IsValid` to return `false` when checking the empty string. In this way, the Assert.IsFalse state-ment plays a double role: as the actual test, and as documentation of the expected behavior. In other words, tests are examples of what the system does.

Writing Tests Make You Write Better Code

Writing tests helps you to write testable code. As a side effect, this leads to code con-sisting of units that are shorter, are simpler, have fewer parameters, and are more loosely coupled (as the guidelines in the previous chapters advise). For example, a method is more difficult to test when it performs multiple functions instead of only one. To make it easier to test, you move responsibilities to different methods, improv-ing the maintainability of the whole. That is why some development approaches advocate writing a unit test before writing the code that conforms to the test. Such approaches are called *test-driven development* (TDD) approaches. You will see that designing a method becomes easier when you think about how you are going to test it: what are the valid arguments of the method, and what should the method return as a result?

10.2 How to Apply the Guideline

How you automate tests differs by the types of tests you want to automate. Test types differ in *what* is tested, by *whom*, and *why*, as detailed in Table 10-1. They are ordered from top to bottom based on the scope of the tests. For example, a unit test has the unit as scope, while an end-to-end test, a regression test, and an acceptance test are on the system level.

Table 10-1. Types of testing

Type	What it tests	Why	Who
Unit test	Functionality of one unit in isolation	Verify that unit behaves as expected	Developer (preferably of the unit)
Integration test	Functionality, performance, or other quality characteristic of at least two classes	Verify that parts of the system work together	Developer
End-to-end test	System interaction (with a user or another system)	Verify that system behaves as expected	Developer
Regression test	Previously erroneous behavior of a unit, class, or system interaction	Ensure that bugs do not re-appear	Developer
Acceptance test	System interaction (with a user or another system)	Confirm the system behaves as required	End-user representative (never the developer)

Table 10-1 shows that a regression test is a unit test, an integration test, or an end-to-end test that has been created when a bug was fixed. Acceptance tests are end-to-end tests executed by end user representatives.

Different types of testing call for different automation frameworks. For unit testing, several well-known C# frameworks are available, such as NUnit (*http://nunit.org*). For automated end-to-end testing, you need a framework that can mimic user input and capture output. A well-known framework that does just that for web development is Selenium (*http://www.seleniumhq.org*). For integration testing, it all depends on the environment in which you are working and the quality characteristics you are testing. SoapUI (*http://www.soapui.org*) is a framework for integration tests that focuses on web services and messaging middleware. Apache jMeter (*http://jmeter.apache.org*) is a framework for testing the performance of C# applications under heavy workloads.

Choosing a test framework needs to be done at the team level. Writing integration tests is a specialized skill—but unit testing is for each and every individual developer. That is why the rest of this chapter focuses on writing unit tests using the most well-known framework for C#: NUnit.

Contrary to specialized integration and end-to-end tests, writing unit tests is a skill that every developer needs to master.

Writing unit tests also requires the smallest upfront investment:[1] just download NUnit from *http://nunit.org*.

Getting Started with NUnit Tests

As we noted in the introduction of this chapter, we want to test IsValid, a method of the class Accounts. Accounts is called the *class under test*. In NUnit, tests are put in a different class, the *test class*, or *test fixture*. This class is indicated as a test fixture by the [TestFixture] attribute. By convention, the name of the test class is the name of the class under test with the suffix Test added. In this case, that would mean the name of the test class is AccountsTest. It must be a public class, but apart from that, there are no other requirements for a test class. In particular, it does not need to extend any other class. It is convenient, but not required, to place the test class in the same namespace as the class under test. That way, the test class has access to all members of the test class under test that have namespace (but not public) access.

In NUnit, a test itself is any method that has the [Test] attribute. To test IsValid, you can use the following NUnit test class:

```
using NUnit.Framework;

namespace eu.sig.training.ch04.v1
{
    [TestFixture]
    public class AccountsTest
    {
        [Test]
        public void TestIsValidNormalCases()
        {
            Assert.IsTrue(Accounts.IsValid("123456789"));
            Assert.IsFalse(Accounts.IsValid("123456788"));
        }

    }
}
```

This test handles two cases:

- Bank account number 123456789: We know this is a valid bank account number (see "The 11-Check for Bank Account Numbers" on page 12), so IsValid should return true. The call of Assert.IsTrue tests this.

---

1 Actually, Visual Studio comes with Microsoft's Unit Testing Framework (*https://msdn.microsoft.com/en-us/library/ms243147(v=vs.90).aspx*), which differs slightly from NUnit.

- Bank account number 123456788: We know this is an invalid bank account number (because it differs from a valid account number by one digit), so `IsValid` should return `false`. The call of Assert.IsFalse tests this.

Unit tests can be run directly in Visual Studio. In addition, NUnit comes with test runners to run tests from the command line. Tests can also be executed by Maven or Ant. Figure 10-1 shows the result of running the preceding test in Visual Studio. The red bar indicates that there are failed tests.

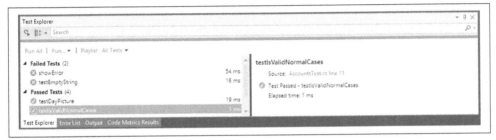

Figure 10-1. All tests succeeded!

The test in the preceding test class only tests normal cases: two bank account numbers of the expected format (exactly nine characters, all digits). How about corner cases? One obvious special case is the empty string. The empty string is, of course, not a valid bank account number, so we test it by calling `Assert.IsFalse`:

```
[Test]
public void TestEmptyString()
{
    Assert.IsFalse(Accounts.IsValid(""));
}
```

As Figure 10-2 shows, it turns out that this test fails! While the call to `IsValid` should return `false`, it actually returned something else (which, of course, must be `true`, as there is no other option).

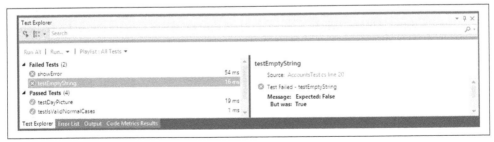

Figure 10-2. One test failed

The failed test points us to a flaw in IsValid. In case the argument to IsValid is the empty string, the for loop does not run at all. So the only lines executed are:

```
int sum = 0;
return sum % 11 == 0;
```

This indeed returns true, while it should return false. This reminds us to add code to IsValid that checks the length of the bank account number.[2]

The NUnit runner reports this as a test *failure* and not as a test *error*. A test *failure* means that the test itself (the method TestEmptyString) is executed perfectly, but the assertion failed. A test *error* means that the test method itself did not execute correctly. The following code snippet illustrates this: the ShowError method raises a division-by-zero exception and never even executes Assert.IsTrue:

```
[Test]
public void ShowError()
{
    int tmp = 0, dummy = 1 / tmp;
    // Next line is never executed because the previous one raises an
    // exception.
    // If it were executed, you'll never see the assert message because
    // the test always succeeds.
    Assert.IsTrue(true);
}
```

Next, we present some basic principles that will help you write good unit tests. We start with the most basic principles and then progress to more advanced ones that apply when your test efforts become more mature.

General Principles for Writing Good Unit Tests

When writing tests, it is important to keep in mind the following general principles:

Test both normal and special cases

As in the examples given in this chapter, test two kinds of cases. Write tests that confirm that a unit indeed behaves as expected on normal input (called *happy flow* or *sunny-side* testing). Also write tests that confirm that a unit behaves sensibly on non-normal input and circumstances (called *unhappy flow* or *rainy-side* testing). For instance, in NUnit it is possible to write tests to confirm that a method under test indeed throws a certain exception.

---

2 And that is still not enough. Because System.GetNumericValue returns -1.0 for a non-numeric character, isValid("72345678z") returns true.

Maintain tests just like nontest (production) code

When you adjust code in the system, the changes should be reflected in the unit tests as well. This is most relevant for unit tests, though it applies to all tests. In particular, when adding new methods or enhancing the behavior of existing methods, be sure to add new test cases that cover that new code.

Write tests that are isolated: their outcomes should reflect only the behavior of the subject being tested

That is, each test should act independently of all other tests. For unit testing, this means that each test case should test only one functionality. No unit test should depend on state, such as files written by other tests. That is why a unit test that, say, causes the class under test to access the filesystem or a database server is not a good unit test.

Consequently, in unit testing you should simulate the state/input of other classes when those are needed (e.g., as arguments). Otherwise, the test is not isolated and would test more than one unit. This was easy for the test of `IsValid`, because `IsValid` takes a string as an argument, and it does not call other methods of our system. For other situations, you may need a technique like *stubbing* or *mocking*.

In Chapter 6, we introduced a C# interface for a simple digital camera, which is repeated here for ease of reference:

```csharp
public interface ISimpleDigitalCamera
{
    Image TakeSnapshot();

    void FlashLightOn();

    void FlashLightOff();
}
```

Suppose this interface is used in an application that ensures people never forget to turn on the flash at night:

```csharp
public const int DAYLIGHT_START = 6;

public Image TakePerfectPicture(int currentHour)
{
    Image image;
    if (currentHour < PerfectPicture.DAYLIGHT_START)
    {
        camera.FlashLightOn();
        image = camera.TakeSnapshot();
        camera.FlashLightOff();
    }
    else
    {
        image = camera.TakeSnapshot();
    }
```

```
        return image;
    }
```

Although the logic is simple (`TakePerfectPicture` simply assumes that if the hour of the day on a 24-hour clock is lower than 6 p.m., it is night), it needs testing. For a proper unit test for `TakePerfectPicture` to be written, taking a picture needs to be automatic and independent. That means that the normal implementation of the digital camera interface cannot be used. On a typical device, the normal implementation requires a (human) user to point the camera at something interesting and press a button. The picture taken can be any picture, so it is hard to test whether the (supposedly perfect) picture taken is the one expected.

The solution is to use an implementation of the camera interface that has been made especially for testing. This implementation is a *fake object*, called a *test stub* or simply a *stub*.[3] In this case, we want this fake object to behave in a preprogrammed (and therefore predictable) way. We write a test stub like this:

```
class DigitalCameraStub : ISimpleDigitalCamera
{
    public Image TestImage;

    public Image TakeSnapshot()
    {
        return this.TestImage;
    }

    public void FlashLightOn()
    {
    }

    public void FlashLightOff()
    {
    }
}
```

In this stub, `TakeSnapshot` always returns the same image, which we can set simply by assigning to `testImage` (for reasons of simplicity, we have made `testImage` a public field and do not provide a setter). This stub can now be used in a test:

```
[Test]
public void TestDayPicture()
{
    Image image =
        Image.FromFile("../../../../test/resources/VanGoghSunflowers.jpg");
    DigitalCameraStub cameraStub = new DigitalCameraStub();
    cameraStub.TestImage = image;
```

---

3 In textbooks and other resources about testing, there is little if any agreement on terminology. We adopt the terminology of *The Art of Unit Testing* by Roy Osherove (Manning Publications, 2009).

```
        PerfectPicture.camera = cameraStub;
        Assert.AreSame(image, new PerfectPicture().TakePerfectPicture(12));
    }
```

In this test, we create a stub camera and supply it with an image to return. We then call TakePerfectPicture(12) and test whether it returns the correct image. The value of the call, 12, means that TakePerfectPicture assumes it is between noon and 1 p.m.

Now suppose we want to test TakePerfectPicture for nighttime behavior; that is, we want to ensure that if TakePerfectPicture is called with a value lower than Perfect Picture.DAYLIGHT_START, it indeed switches on the flash. So, we want to test whether TakePerfectPicture indeed calls FlashLightOn. However, FlashLightOn does not return any value, and the ISimpleDigitalCamera interface also does not provide any other way to know whether the flash has been switched on. So what to check?

The solution is to provide the fake digital camera implementation with some mechanism to record whether the method we are interested in gets called. A fake object that records whether expected calls have taken place is called a *mock object*. So, a mock object is a stub object with added test-specific behavior. The digital camera mock object looks like this:

```
class DigitalCameraMock : ISimpleDigitalCamera
{
    public Image TestImage;
    public int FlashOnCounter = 0;

    public Image TakeSnapshot()
    {
        return this.TestImage;
    }

    public void FlashLightOn()
    {
        this.FlashOnCounter++;
    }

    public void FlashLightOff()
    {
    }
}
```

Compared to DigitalCameraStub, DigitalCameraMock additionally keeps track of the number of times FlashLightOn has been called, in a public field. DigitalCamera Mock still contains preprogrammed behavior, so it is both a stub and a mock. We can check that FlashLightOn is called in the unit test like so:

```
[Test]
public void TestNightPicture()
{
```

```
    Image image =
        Image.FromFile("../../../../test/resources/VanGoghStarryNight.jpg");
    DigitalCameraMock cameraMock = new DigitalCameraMock();
    cameraMock.TestImage = image;
    PerfectPicture.camera = cameraMock;
    Assert.AreSame(image, new PerfectPicture().TakePerfectPicture(0));
    Assert.AreEqual(1, cameraMock.FlashOnCounter);
}
```

In these examples, we have written our own stub and mock objects. This leads to a lot of code. Generally, it is most efficient to use a *mocking framework* such as Moq (*https://github.com/Moq/moq4*). Mocking frameworks use features of the .Net runtime to automatically create mock objects from normal interfaces or classes. They also provide methods to test whether methods of a mock object have been called, and with which arguments. Some mocking frameworks also provide ways to specify preprogrammed behavior of mock objects, giving them the characteristics of both stubs and mocks.

Indeed, using Moq as an example, you can write `TestNightPicture` without any need to write a class like `DigitalCameraMock` yourself:

```
[Test]
public void TestNightPictureMoq()
{
    Image image =
        Image.FromFile("../../../../test/resources/VanGoghStarryNight.jpg");
    var cameraMock = new Mock<ISimpleDigitalCamera>();
    cameraMock.Setup(foo => foo.TakeSnapshot()).Returns(image);
    PerfectPicture.camera = cameraMock.Object;
    Assert.AreSame(image, new PerfectPicture().TakePerfectPicture(0));
    cameraMock.Verify(foo => foo.FlashLightOn(), Times.AtMostOnce());
}
```

In this test, Moq's `Mock` constructor is used to create `cameraMock`, the mock object used in this test. With Moq's `Setup` and `Returns` method, the desired behavior is specified. Moq's `Verify` method is used to verify whether `FlashLightOn` has been called.

Measure Coverage to Determine Whether There Are Enough Tests

How many unit tests are needed? One way to assess whether you have written enough unit tests is to measure *coverage* of your unit tests. Coverage, or more precisely, line coverage, is the percentage of lines of code in your codebase that actually get executed when all unit tests are executed. As a rule of thumb, you should aim for *at least 80% line coverage with a sufficient number of tests—that is, as many lines of test code as production code.*

Why 80% coverage (and not 100%)? Any codebase contains fragments of trivial code that technically can be tested, but are so trivial that testing them makes little sense. Take the following typical C# getter method:

```
public string Name { get; }
```

It is possible to test this getter (with something like `Assert.AreEq ual(myObj.Name,"John Smith")`), but with this test, you are mostly testing that the C# compiler and the .Net runtime work as expected. But it is not true that you should never test getters. Take a typical class that represents postal mail addresses. It typically has two or three string fields that represent (additional) address lines. It is easy to make a mistake like this one:

```
public string getAddressLine3() {
    return this.addressLine2;
}
```

A minimum of 80% coverage alone is not enough to ensure high-quality unit tests. It is possible to get high coverage by testing just a few high-level methods (like `Main`, the first method called by the .NET runtime) and *not* mock out lower-level methods. That is why we advise a 1-to-1 ratio of production code versus test code.

You can measure coverage using a code coverage tool. Some editions of Visual Studio provide a built-in code coverage tool. Figure 10-3 shows coverage of the examples of this book, using Visual Studio 2015 Enterprise Edition.

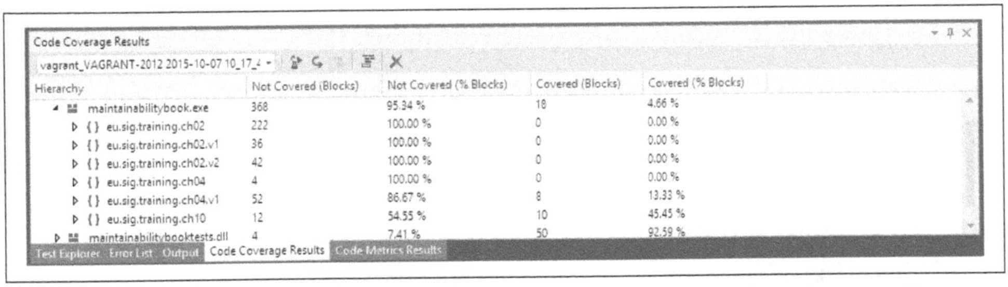

Figure 10-3. Coverage report of the examples of this book in Visual Studio 2015 Enterprise Edition.

10.3 Common Objections to Automating Tests

This section discusses typical objections and limitations regarding automation. They deal with the reasons and considerations to invest in test automation.

Objection: We Still Need Manual Testing

"Why should we invest in automated tests at all if we still need manual testing?"

The answer to this question is simply because test automation frees up time to manually test those things that cannot be automated.

Consider the downsides of the alternative to automated tests. Manual testing has clear limitations. It is slow, expensive, and hard to repeat in a consistent manner. In fact, technical verification of the system *needs* to take place anyway, since you cannot manually test code that does not work. Because manual tests are not easily repeatable, even with small code changes a full retest may be needed to be sure that the system works as intended.

Manual acceptance testing can largely be automated with automated regression tests. With those, the scope of remaining manual tests decreases. You may still need manual review or acceptance tests to verify that *business logic* is correct. This typically concerns the process flow of a functionality.

Objection: I Am Not Allowed to Write Unit Tests

"I am not allowed to write unit tests because they lower productivity according to my manager."

Writing unit tests during development actually improves productivity. It improves system code by shifting the focus from "what code should do" toward "what it should not do." If you never take into account how the code may fail, you cannot be sure whether your code is resilient to unexpected situations.

The disadvantages of not having unit tests are mainly in uncertainty and rework. Every time a piece of code is changed, it requires painstaking review to verify whether the code does what it is supposed to do.

Objection: Why Should We Invest in Unit Tests When the Current Coverage Is Low?

"The current unit test coverage of my system is very low. Why should I invest time now in writing unit tests?"

We have elaborated on the reasons why unit tests are useful and help you develop code that works predictably. However, when a very large system has little to no unit test code, this may be a burden. After all, it would be a significant investment to start writing unit tests from scratch for an existing system because you would need to analyze all units again. Therefore, you should make a significant investment in unit tests only if the added certainty is worth the effort. This especially applies to critical, central functionality and when there is reason to believe that units are behaving in an unintended manner. Otherwise, add unit tests incrementally each time you change existing code or add new code.

In general, when the unit test coverage of a system is much below the industry best practice of 80%, a good strategy is to apply the "Boy Scout rule." This rule says to leave code in a better state than you found it (see also Chapter 12 on applying this principle). Thus, when you are adjusting code, you have the opportunity to (re)write unit tests to ensure that in the new state, the code is still working as expected.

10.4 See Also

Standardization and consistency in applying it are important in achieving a well-automated development environment. For elaboration, see Chapter 11.

How SIG Rates Testability

Testability is one of the five subcharacteristics of maintainability according to ISO 25010. SIG rates testability by aggregating the ratings of system properties *unit complexity* (see Chapter 3), *component independence* (see Chapter 7), and *system volume* (see Chapter 9), using an aggregation mechanism as explained in Appendix A.

The rationale for this is that complex units are especially hard to test, poor component independence increases the need for mocking and stubbing, and higher volumes of production code require higher volumes of test code.

CHAPTER 11

Write Clean Code

Writing clean code is what you must do in order to call yourself a professional.

—Robert C. Martin

Guideline:

- **Write clean code**.
- Do this by **not leaving code smells behind** after development work.
- This improves maintainability because **clean code is maintainable code**.

Code smells are coding patterns that hint that a problem is present. Introducing or not removing such patterns is bad practice, as they decrease the maintainability of code. In this chapter we discuss guidelines for keeping the codebase clean from code smells to achieve a "hygienic environment."

11.1 Leave No Trace

Boy Scouts have a rule that says, "leave the campground cleaner than you found it." Applying the Boy Scout rule to software development means that once you are writing or modifying a piece of code, you have the opportunity to make small improvements as well. The result is that you leave the code cleaner and more maintainable than you found it. If you are adjusting a piece of code now, apparently there is a need for maintaining it. That increases the chance that you will revisit that same code later. When you revisit that code again, you will benefit from the refactoring you are doing now.

11.2 How to Apply the Guideline

Trying to be a clean coder is an ambitious goal, and there are many best practices that you can follow. From our consultancy experience we have distilled seven developer "Boy Scout rules" that will help you to prevent code smells that impact maintainability most:

1. Leave no unit-level code smells behind.
2. Leave no bad comments behind.
3. Leave no code in comments behind.
4. Leave no dead code behind.
5. Leave no long identifier names behind.
6. Leave no magic constants behind.
7. Leave no badly handled exceptions behind.

These seven rules are explained in the following sections.

Rule 1: Leave No-Unit Level Code Smells Behind

At this point in the book you are familiar with nine guidelines for building maintainable software, discussed in the previous nine chapters. Of those nine guidelines, three deal with smells at the unit level: long units (Chapter 2), complex units (Chapter 3), and units with large interfaces (Chapter 5). For modern programming languages, there is really no good reason why any of these guidelines should be violated when you are writing new code.

To follow this rule is to refactor "smelly" code in time. By "*in time*," we mean as soon as possible but certainly before the code is committed to the version control system. Of course, it is OK to have small violations when you are working on a development ticket—for example, a method of 20 lines of code or a method with 5 parameters. But these violations should be refactored out before you commit your changes.

Of course, the other guidelines, such as avoiding duplicated code and preventing tight coupling, are equally important to building a maintainable system. However, as a responsible software developer, you will find the first three guidelines are easy to integrate with your daily way of working. Violations of unit length, complexity, and parameters are easy to detect. It is very common to have these checks available in modern integrated development environments. We actually advise you to turn on this feature and make sure your code is free from unit-level code smells before each commit.

Rule 2: Leave No Bad Comments Behind

Comments are sometimes considered the anti-pattern of good code. From our experience we can confirm that inline comments typically indicate a lack of elegant engineering solutions. Consider the following method taken from the Jenkins codebase (which is in Java):

```java
public HttpResponse doUploadPlugin(StaplerRequest req)
    throws IOException, ServletException {
    try {
        Jenkins.getInstance().checkPermission(UPLOAD_PLUGINS);

        ServletFileUpload upload = new ServletFileUpload(
            new DiskFileItemFactory());

        // Parse the request
        FileItem fileItem = (FileItem)upload.parseRequest(req).get(0);
        String fileName = Util.getFileName(fileItem.getName());
        if ("".equals(fileName)) {
            return new HttpRedirect("advanced");
        }
        // we allow the upload of the new jpi's and the legacy hpi's
        if (!fileName.endsWith(".jpi") && !fileName.endsWith(".hpi")) {
            throw new Failure("Not a plugin: " + fileName);
        }

        // first copy into a temporary file name
        File t = File.createTempFile("uploaded", ".jpi");
        t.deleteOnExit();
        fileItem.write(t);
        fileItem.delete();

        final String baseName = identifyPluginShortName(t);

        pluginUploaded = true;

        // Now create a dummy plugin that we can dynamically load
        // (the InstallationJob will force a restart if one is needed):
        JSONObject cfg = new JSONObject().element("name", baseName)
            .element("version", "0"). // unused but mandatory
            element("url", t.toURI().toString())
            .element("dependencies", new JSONArray());
        new UpdateSite(UpdateCenter.ID_UPLOAD, null).new Plugin(
            UpdateCenter.ID_UPLOAD, cfg).deploy(true);
        return new HttpRedirect("../updateCenter");
    } catch (IOException e) {
        throw e;
    } catch (Exception e) {// grrr. fileItem.write throws this
        throw new ServletException(e);
    }
}
```

Although the `doUploadPlugin` is not very hard to maintain (it has only 1 parameter, 32 lines of code, and a McCabe index of 6), the inline comments indicate separate concerns that could easily be addressed outside this method. For example, copying the `fileItem` to a temporary file and creating the plugin configuration are tasks that deserve their own methods (where they can be tested and potentially reused).

Comments in code may reveal many different problems:

- Lack of understanding of the code itself

  ```
  // I don't know what is happening here, but if I remove this line
  // an infinite loop occurs
  ```

- Issue tracking systems not properly used

  ```
  // JIRA-1234: Fixes a bug when summing negative numbers
  ```

- Conventions or tooling are being bypassed

  ```
  // CHECKSTYLE:OFF
  // NOPMD
  ```

- Good intentions

  ```
  // TODO: Make this method a lot faster some day
  ```

Comments are valuable in only a small number of cases. Helpful API documentation can be such a case, but always be cautious to avoid dogmatic boilerplate commentary. In general, the best advice we can give is to keep your code free of comments.

Rule 3: Leave No Code in Comments Behind

Although there might be rare occasions where there is a good reason to use comments in your code, there is never an excuse for checking in code that is commented out. The version control system will always keep a record of old code, so it is perfectly safe to delete it. Take a look at the following example, taken from the Apache Tomcat codebase (which is in Java, but we present a C# translation here):

```csharp
private void ValidateFilterMap(FilterMap filterMap) {
    // Validate the proposed filter mapping
    string filterName = filterMap.GetFilterName();
    string[] servletNames = filterMap.GetServletNames();
    string[] urlPatterns = filterMap.GetURLPatterns();
    if (FindFilterDef(filterName) == null)
        throw new Exception(
            sm.GetString("standardContext.filterMap.name", filterName));

    if (!filterMap.GetMatchAllServletNames() &&
        !filterMap.GetMatchAllUrlPatterns() &&
        (servletNames.Length == 0) && (urlPatterns.Length == 0))
        throw new Exception(
            sm.GetString("standardContext.filterMap.either"));
```

```
        // FIXME: Older spec revisions may still check this
        /*
        if ((servletNames.length != 0) && (urlPatterns.length != 0))
            throw new IllegalArgumentException
                (sm.getString("standardContext.filterMap.either"));
        */
        for (int i = 0; i < urlPatterns.Length; i++) {
            if (!ValidateURLPattern(urlPatterns[i])) {
                throw new Exception(
                    sm.GetString("standardContext.filterMap.pattern",
                        urlPatterns[i]));
            }
        }
    }
```

The FIXME note and accompanying code are understandable from the original developer's perspective, but to a new developer they act as a distractor. The original developer had to make a decision before leaving this commented-out code: either fix it at the spot, create a new ticket to fix it at some other time, or reject this corner case altogether.

Rule 4: Leave No Dead Code Behind

Dead code comes in different shapes. Dead code is code that is not executed at all or its output is "dead": the code may be executed, but its output is not used elsewhere in the system. Code in comments, as discussed in the previous section, is an example of dead code, but there are many other forms of dead code. In this section, we give three more examples of dead code.

Unreachable code in methods

```
    public Transaction GetTransaction(long uid)
    {
        Transaction result = new Transaction(uid);
        if (result != null)
        {
            return result;
        }
        else
        {
            return LookupTransaction(uid); ❶
        }
    }
```

❶   Unreachable code

Unused private methods

Private methods can be called only from other code in the same class. If they are not, they are dead code. Nonprivate methods that are not called by methods in the same class may also be dead, but you cannot determine this by looking at the code of the class alone.

Code in comments

This is not to be confused with commented-out code. Sometimes it can be useful to use short code snippets in API documentation (such as in C# XMLDOC tags), but remember that keeping those snippets in sync with the actual code is a task that is quickly overlooked. Avoid code in comments if possible.

Rule 5: Leave No Long Identifiers Behind

Good identifiers make all the difference between code that is a pleasure to read and code that is hard to wrap your head around. A famous saying by Phil Karlton is "There are only two hard problems in computer science: cache invalidation and naming things." In this book we won't discuss the first, but we do want to say a few things about long identifiers.

Identifiers name the items in your codebase, from units to modules to components to even the system itself. It is important to choose good names so that developers can find their way through the codebase without great effort. The names of most of the identifiers in a codebase will be dependent on the domain in which the system operates. It is typical for teams to have a formal naming convention or an informal, but consistent, use of domain-specific terminology.

It is not easy to choose the right identifiers in your code, and unfortunately there are no guidelines for what is and what isn't a good identifier. Sometimes it may even take you a couple of iterations to find the right name for a method or class.

As a general rule, long identifiers must be avoided. A maximum length for an identifier is hard to define (some domains have longer terminology than others), but in most cases there is little debate within a development team when an identifier is considered too long. Identifiers that express multiple responsibilities (such as `generate ConsoleAnnotationScriptAndStylesheet`) or contain too many technical terms (e.g., `GlobalProjectNamingStrategyConfiguration`) are always a violation of this rule.

Rule 6: Leave No Magic Constants Behind

Magic constants are number or literal values that are used in code without a clear definition of their meaning (hence the name *magic* constant). Consider the following code example:

```
float CalculateFare(Customer c, long distance)
{
    float travelledDistanceFare = distance * 0.10f;
    if (c.Age < 12)
    {
        travelledDistanceFare *= 0.25f;
    }
    else
        if (c.Age >= 65)
    {
        travelledDistanceFare *= 0.5f;
    }
    return 3.00f + travelledDistanceFare;
}
```

All the numbers in this code example could be considered magic numbers. For instance, the age thresholds for children and the elderly may seem like familiar numbers, but remember they could be used at many other places in the codebase. The fare rates are constants that are likely to change over time by business demands.

The next snippet shows what the code looks like if we define all magic constants explicitly. The code volume increased with six extra lines of code, which is a lot compared to the original source, but remember that these constants can be reused in many other places in the code:

```
private static readonly float BASE_RATE = 3.00f;
private static readonly float FARE_PER_KM = 0.10f;
private static readonly float DISCOUNT_RATE_CHILDREN = 0.25f;
private static readonly float DISCOUNT_RATE_ELDERLY = 0.5f;
private static readonly int MAXIMUM_AGE_CHILDREN = 12;
private static readonly int MINIMUM_AGE_ELDERLY = 65;

float CalculateFare(Customer c, long distance)
{
    float travelledDistanceFare = distance * FARE_PER_KM;
    if (c.Age < MAXIMUM_AGE_CHILDREN)
    {
        travelledDistanceFare *= DISCOUNT_RATE_CHILDREN;
    }
    else
        if (c.Age >= MINIMUM_AGE_ELDERLY)
    {
        travelledDistanceFare *= DISCOUNT_RATE_ELDERLY;
    }
```

```
    return BASE_RATE + travelledDistanceFare;
}
```

Rule 7: Leave No Badly Handled Exception Behind

Three guidelines for good exception handling are discussed here specifically because in our practice we see many flaws in implementing exception handling:

- **Always catch exceptions.** You are logging failures of the system to help you understand these failures and then improve the system's reaction to them. That means that exceptions must always be caught. Also, in some cases an empty `catch` block compiles, but it is bad practice since it does not provide information about the context of the exception.

- **Catch specific exceptions.** To make exceptions traceable to a specific event, you should catch specific exceptions. General exceptions that do not provide information specific to the state or event that triggered it fail to provide that traceability. Therefore, you should not catch `Exception` or `SystemException` directly.

- **Translate specific exceptions to general messages before showing them to end users.** End users should not be "bothered" with detailed exceptions, since they are mostly confusing and a security bad practice (i.e., providing more information than necessary about the inner workings of the system).

11.3 Common Objections to Writing Clean Code

This section discusses typical objections regarding clean code. The most common objections are reasons why commenting would be a good way to document code and whether corners can be cut for doing exception handling.

Objection: Comments Are Our Documentation

"We use comments to document the workings of the code."

Comments that tell the truth can be a valuable aid to less experienced developers who want to understand how a piece of code works. In practice, however, most comments in code lie—not on purpose, of course, but comments often tell an outdated version of the truth. Outdated comments become more and more common as the system gets older. Keeping comments in sync with code is a task that requires precision and a lot of times is overlooked during maintenance.

Code that "tells the story" itself does not require lengthy comments to document its workings. By keeping units small and simple, and by using descriptive names for identifiers, using comments for documentation is seldom necessary.

Objection: Exception Handling Causes Code Additions

"Implementing exception classes forces me to add a lot of extra code without visible benefits."

Exception handling is an important part of *defensive programming*: coding to prevent unstable situations and unpredictable system behavior. Anticipating unstable situations means trying to foresee what can go wrong. This does indeed add to the burden of analysis and coding. However, this is an investment. The benefits of exception handling may not be visible now, but they definitely will prove valuable in preventing and absorbing unstable situations in the future.

By defining exceptions, you are documenting and safeguarding your assumptions. They can later be adjusted when circumstances change.

Objection: Why Only These Coding Guidelines?

"We use a much longer list of coding conventions and quality checks in our team. This list of seven seems like an arbitrary selection with many important omissions."

Having more guidelines and checks than the seven in this chapter is of course not a problem. These seven rules are the ones we consider the most important for writing maintainable code and the ones that should be adhered to by every member on the development team. A risk of having many guidelines and checks is that developers can be overwhelmed by them and focus their efforts on the less critical issues. However, teams are obviously allowed to extend this list with items that they find indispensable for building a maintainable system.

CHAPTER 12

Next Steps

At this point, you know a lot more about what maintainable code is, why it is important, and how to apply the 10 guidelines in this book. But writing maintainable code is not something you learn from a book. You learn it by doing it! Therefore, here we will discuss simple advice on practicing the 10 guidelines for achieving maintainable software.

12.1 Turning the Guidelines into Practice

Ensuring that your code is easy to maintain depends on two behaviors in your daily routine: *discipline* and *setting priorities*. Discipline helps you to constantly keep improving your coding techniques, up to a point where any new code you write will already be maintainable. As for priorities, some of the presented guidelines can seem to contradict each other. It takes consideration on your side about which guideline has the most impact on the actual maintainability of your system. Be sure to take some time to deliberate and ask your team for their opinion.

12.2 Lower-Level (Unit) Guidelines Take Precedence Over Higher-Level (Component) Guidelines

Keep in mind that the aggregated higher-level guidelines are effects of the application applying the lower-level principles. For example, when units of code are long and duplicated throughout the system (see Chapters 2 and 4), the codebase will likely be large as well (see Chapter 9). This is because one of the causes of having a large codebase is that long units are being duplicated.

Therefore, when there is a conflict between two guidelines, adhering to the lower-level guidelines leads to better overall system maintainability. For instance, splitting units into multiple smaller units slightly grows the total codebase. But the advantage of small units in terms of reusability will have a huge pay-off when more functionality is added to the system.

The same applies to the architecture-level guidelines (see Chapters 7 and 8): it makes no sense to reorganize your code structure when it makes your components highly dependent on each other. To put it succinctly: fix your dependencies before trying to balance your components.

12.3 Remember That Every Commit Counts

The hardest part of applying the guidelines in this book may be keeping the discipline to apply them. It is tempting to violate the guidelines when a "quick fix" seems more efficient. To keep this discipline, follow the *Boy Scout rule* presented in Chapter 11.

The Boy Scout rule is especially effective on large codebases. Unless you have the time to sort out your whole system and improve maintainability, you will have to do it step-by-step while doing your regular work. This gradually improves maintainability and hones your refactoring skills. So, in the long run, you also have the skill to write highly maintainable software.

12.4 Development Process Best Practices Are Discussed in the Follow-Up Book

As discussed in the preface, the *process* part of developing high-quality software is discussed in detail in the follow-up book in this series: *Building Software Teams*. It provides 10 guidelines for managing and measuring the software development process. It focuses on how to measure and manage best practices for software development (e.g., development tool support, automation, standardization).

How SIG Measures Maintainability

SIG measures system maintainability based on eight metrics. Those eight metrics are discussed in Chapters 2 through 9. Those chapters include sidebars explaining how SIG rates source code properties relevant to those guidelines. These ratings are derived from the SIG/TÜViT[1] Evaluation Criteria for Trusted Product Maintainability. In this appendix, we provide you with additional background.

Together with TÜViT, SIG has determined eight properties of source code that can be measured automatically. See "Why These Ten Specific Guidelines?" on page xi for how these properties have been chosen.

To assess maintainability of a system, we measure these eight source code properties and summarize these measurements either in a single number (for instance, the percentage of code duplication) or a couple of numbers (for instance, the percentage of code in four categories of complexity, which we call a quality profile; see "Rating Maintainability").

We then compare these numbers against a benchmark containing several hundreds of systems, using Table A-1 to determine the quality level on each property. So, if the measurement for a system is among the top 5% of all systems in the benchmark, the system is rated at 5 stars for this property. If it is among the next best 30%, it rates 4 stars, and so forth. This process of comparing quality profiles for each system property against the benchmark results in eight star ratings, one for each system property.

---

1 TÜViT is part of TÜV, a worldwide organization of German origin for technical quality management. It specializes in certification and consulting of IT in general and security in particular.

Table A-1. SIG maintainability ratings

Rating	Maintainability
5 stars	Top 5% of the systems in the benchmark
4 stars	Next 30% of the systems in the benchmark (above-average systems)
3 stars	Next 30% of the systems in the benchmark (average systems)
2 stars	Next 30% of the systems in the benchmark (below-average systems)
1 star	Bottom 5% least maintainable systems

We then aggregate the ratings to arrive at one overall rating. We do this in two steps. First, we determine the ratings for the subcharacteristics of maintainability as defined by ISO 25010 (i.e., analyzability, modifiability, etc.) by taking the weighted averages according to the rows of Table A-2. Each cross in a given row indicates that the corresponding system property (column) contributes to this subcharacteristic. Second, we take a weighted average of the five subcharacteristics to determine an overall rating for maintainability.

Table A-2. Relation of subcharacteristics and system properties

	Volume	Duplication	Unit size	Unit complexity	Unit interfacing	Module coupling	Component balance	Component independence
Analyzability	X	X	X				X	
Modifiability		X		X		X		
Testability	X			X				X
Modularity						X	X	X
Reusability			X		X			

This describes the SIG maintainability model in a nutshell, since there is more detail to it than what we can cover in this appendix. If you would like to learn more about the details of the maintainability model, a good start for elaboration is the following publication:

- Visser, Joost. *SIG/TÜViT Evaluation Criteria Trusted Product Maintainability.* http://bit.ly/eval_criteria

Background on the development of the model and its application is provided in the following publications:

- Heitlager, Ilja, Tobias Kuipers, and Joost Visser. "A Practical Model for Measuring Maintainability." In *Proceedings of the 6th International Conference on the Quality of Information and Communications Technology (QUATIC 2007)*, 30–39. IEEE Computer Society Press, 2007.
- Baggen, Robert, José Pedro Correia, Katrin Schill, and Joost Visser. "Standardized code quality benchmarking for improving software maintainability." *Software Quality Journal* 20, no. 2 (2012): 287–307.
- Bijlsma, Dennis, Miguel Alexandre Ferreira, Bart Luijten, and Joost Visser. "Faster issue resolution with higher technical quality of software." *Software Quality Journal* 20, no. 2 (2012): 265–285.

Does Maintainability Improve Over Time?

A question we often get at SIG is whether maintainability improves over time across all systems we see. The answer is yes, but very slowly. The recalibration that we carry out every year consistently shows that the thresholds become stricter over time. This means that for one system to get a high maintainability rating, over time it must have fewer units that are overly long or complex, must have less duplication, lower coupling, and so on. Given the structure of our model, the reason for this must be that systems in our benchmark over time have less duplication, less tight coupling, and so on. One could argue that this means that maintainability across the systems we acquire for our benchmark is improving. We are not talking about big changes. In broad terms, we can say this: it is about a tenth of a star per year.

The selection of systems within the SIG benchmark is a representative cross-cut of the software industry, including both proprietary and open source systems, developed in a variety of languages, functional domains, platforms, and so on. Therefore, the tenth of a star improvement per year means that the industry as a whole is slowly but constantly improving.

Index

Colophon

The animal on the cover of *Building Maintainable Software* is a grey-headed wood-pecker (*Picus canus*). Like all woodpeckers, which consitute about half of the Pici-formes order, grey-headed woodpeckers use strong bills to puncture the surface of trees and seek small insects that inhabit the wood. Very long, bristly tongues coated with an adhesive extend into deep cracks, holes, and crevices to gather food in the bird's bill. A membrane that closes over the woodpecker's eye protects it from the debris that may result from each blow at the tree. Slit-like nostrils provide a similar protection, as do feathers that cover them. Adaptations to the brain like small size and a position that maximizes its contact with the skull—permitting optimal shock absorption—represent further guards against the violence of the woodpecker's drill-ing. The zygodactyl arrangement of the feet, putting two toes forward and two back, allow the woodpecker to maintain its position on the tree's trunk during this activity, as well as to traverse vertically up and down it.

Grey-headed woodpeckers maintain a vast range across Eurasia, though individual members of the species tend to be homebodies to particular forest and woodland habitats. As such, they rarely travel overseas and switch to a seed-based diet in winter. Mating calls that begin with high-pitched whistles lead to monogamous pairs roost-ing with clutches of 5 to 10 eggs in the holes that males bore into the trunks of trees, where both parents remain to incubate eggs and nurse the hatchlings for the three to four weeks in which the hatchlings progress to juveniles. At this point, the young can fly from the nest and gather their own food.

In their greenish back and tail plumage, grey-headed woodpeckers very much resem-ble the closely related green woodpecker, and males of the species will develop on their foreheads the red patch that appears on many other species of woodpecker.

Many of the animals on O'Reilly covers are endangered; all of them are important to the world. To learn more about how you can help, go to *animals.oreilly.com*.

The cover image is from Lydekker's *Royal Natural History*. The cover fonts are URW Typewriter and Guardian Sans. The text font is Adobe Minion Pro; the heading font is Adobe Myriad Condensed; and the code font is Dalton Maag's Ubuntu Mono.

Get even more for your money.

Join the O'Reilly Community, and register the O'Reilly books you own. It's free, and you'll get:

- $4.99 ebook upgrade offer
- 40% upgrade offer on O'Reilly print books
- Membership discounts on books and events
- Free lifetime updates to ebooks and videos
- Multiple ebook formats, DRM FREE
- Participation in the O'Reilly community
- Newsletters
- Account management
- 100% Satisfaction Guarantee

Signing up is easy:

1. Go to: oreilly.com/go/register
2. Create an O'Reilly login.
3. Provide your address.
4. Register your books.

Note: English-language books only

To order books online:
oreilly.com/store

For questions about products or an order:
orders@oreilly.com

To sign up to get topic-specific email announcements and/or news about upcoming books, conferences, special offers, and new technologies:
elists@oreilly.com

For technical questions about book content:
booktech@oreilly.com

To submit new book proposals to our editors:
proposals@oreilly.com

O'Reilly books are available in multiple DRM-free ebook formats. For more information:
oreilly.com/ebooks